FELICIA CARTRIGHT

AND THE CASE OF THE
LOST PUPPY

Felicia   Joan

FELICIA CARTRIGHT

AND THE CASE OF THE
LOST PUPPY

BERNARD PALMER

Aneko Press Youth

www.anekopress.com

Aneko Press, Life Sentence Publishing, and our logos are trademarks of
Life Sentence Publishing, Inc.
203 E. Birch Street
P.O. Box 652
Abbotsford, WI 54405

JUVENILE FICTION / Religious / Christian / Action & Adventure

Paperback ISBN: 979-8-88936-306-4

eBook ISBN: 979-8-88936-307-1

10 9 8 7 6 5 4 3 2 1

Available where books are sold

CONTENTS

CHAPTER 1

"DANIEL L. JULIAN, PROP."

Miss Amelia Duncan, dean of Wellington School for Girls, whirled her white Volkswagen expertly around the sharp Ozark Mountain corner and pressed the accelerator. Only then did she glance at the blond-haired girl to her right.

"Felicia, you watch your side of the road."

Felicia Cartright nodded. "Yes, Miss Duncan."

"Joan," she said to her passenger in the rear seat.

There was no answer.

"Joan," she repeated, her voice rising, "are you asleep again?"

Joan Bailey sat up with a start.

"Yes, Miss Duncan. I mean no, Miss Duncan. I–" Her voice died helplessly.

A dry wisp of laughter escaped the austere dean's lips.

Ever since they had left Wellington School for

Girls at the close of the spring term and had driven west, Miss Duncan had been unbending a little more.

"Know something, Felicia," Joan had whispered only the night before, "I do believe she's human after all."

Miss Duncan's laughter was soft and musical.

"Joan, I want you to stay awake and watch on your side of the road. We surely will be seeing the sign Ingrid Steffins wrote about before long."

"That's what we've been saying for the last fifty miles," Joan answered. "I've been wondering if there is such a cave."

Miss Duncan's mouth tightened to the thin steel-hard line they had grown accustomed to at school.

"That little girl wrote that we could follow the signs. There are signs to follow. You can be sure of that."

"But where are they?" Joan persisted. "That's what I want to know."

"Miss Bailey." Miss Duncan became the dean once more. "Miss Bailey, if I knew where the signs were, I would find them myself. I would not have you looking for them."

Felicia Cartright, who had been sitting silently beside Miss Duncan, leaned forward.

"There's a sign advertising a cave," she said.

Automatically, the driver slowed.

"'Constellation Cave,'" Felicia read aloud, "'the Eighth Wonder of the World.'"

Joan Bailey giggled.

"Wrong cave. We're looking for 'Colossal Cave, the Greatest Scenic Attraction in the Ozarks.'"

"Your memory has served you well, Joan," Miss Duncan said. "What a pity you never use it on Latin or English Literature."

Joan laughed good-naturedly. "I would, Miss Duncan, but I don't want to wear it out."

"I don't want you to wear out your eyes, either, but do keep them open until we see that sign."

* * *

The Ozark Mountains had not been included in the itinerary when Miss Duncan, Felicia, and Joan planned their trip to California at the close of the school year. But, as the dean of Wellington was making arrangements for the trip, a letter came to her desk from twelve-year-old Ingrid Steffins. She read it over several times and called the girls to her office.

"I'd like to have you both read this letter."

Joan Bailey took it first.

"She sounds like a sweet little girl. How did she get your name, Miss Duncan?"

"She explains that in the letter. She got it from one of our Wellington girls. I can't imagine what the girl's maiden name was, but Ingrid said that she is married to her former pastor."

Felicia read the letter carefully.

"It would be fun to stop by and visit her, wouldn't it?"

"Her family operates a sightseeing cave," Joan said. "For some reason that intrigues me."

"I wasn't thinking of our visit as being intriguing," Miss Duncan announced primly, "or interesting or even fun. This poor child is the only Christian in her family. Our stopping by could be a real encouragement to her."

"I hadn't thought of that," Felicia said.

"And besides," Miss Duncan replied, her eyes twinkling, "I've often wondered what it would be like to stay with a family that operated a cave myself."

* * *

Several miles up the road, Joan Bailey saw another sign advertising Constellation Cave.

"You don't suppose her dad changed the cave's name, do you?"

"That hardly seems likely."

"We're eighteen or twenty miles out of Lodgeville, aren't we?" Felicia asked.

Miss Duncan nodded her agreement. "That's right. And, as I recall, Ingrid's last letter said that's about the distance she and her parents live from town."

"Then we must be getting close," Joan Bailey put in.

"Here's another sign for Constellation Cave," Miss Duncan said. "If we aren't at the right place, the chances are the proprietor can direct us to the Steffins' establishment."

She reduced speed as they approached the driveway with the big arrow pointing at right angles to the highway and turned in. The house was small and completely devoid of paint. The screen door sagged on its hinges, and the bottom porch step was broken. The barn was even more decrepit than the house. The roof ridge sagged wearily in the middle. It had once been shingled, but that had been a long time ago. The building listed toward the road, and the barn door, half open, looked as though it had not been closed for years.

Splitting the distance between the two main buildings was a tiny edition of a house, identified by a huge sign on top. "Constellation Cave. Souvenirs. Tickets here." And on the door was a smaller sign. "If closed, ring bell."

Against the base of the mountain fifty or sixty yards away stood still another building constructed with the same haphazard workmanship. "Constellation Cave. The Eighth Wonder of the World. Guided Tours 8 to 6 o'clock every day or by appointment. Daniel L. Julian, Prop."

Miss Duncan braked to a stop before the shop where tickets and souvenirs were sold.

"Well, do you suppose this Daniel L. Julian will know where the Steffins family lives?" she murmured.

Joan Bailey laughed pleasantly. "We'll never find out sitting in here."

"Quite so."

Miss Duncan got out of the car stiffly, for they had been riding a long while, and started up the steps. She was reaching for the door when a man's voice boomed to her. "Just a minute, lady. I'll take care of you."

She turned to see a big, burly man, whose stomach pushed out his overalls until the buttons on each side threatened to pop off, come waddling down the house steps. As he did so, he wiped his hands on the bib of his overalls and gulped a last morsel of food.

"You ladies stopped at the right place," he said. "This here's the most wonderful cave in all the world."

As he came closer, Miss Duncan saw that his face bristled with whiskers, and he hadn't had a haircut for about two months. She wrinkled her nose distastefully.

"We've had kings of Egypt stop here and say that they ain't never seen nothin' like our cave. They said it was better'n the pyramids."

"That must have been a long while ago, my good man," Miss Duncan informed him. The schoolteacher in her would not be still at such blatant misinformation. "It has been many, many years since King Farouk of Egypt was overthrown."

That stopped him but only for a moment.

"I don't remember for sure where that there king

was from. He was from Egypt or New Guinea or Australia or one of them European countries. Anyway, he says we've got 'em all beat when it comes to caves."

Miss Duncan straightened.

"I am sure it is well worth our time to go through your cave," she said. "However, today we have just stopped for a little information."

A scowl spread across his heavy, jowled face.

"What ya wanta know?"

"We are looking for a family by the name of Steffins. They own and operate Colossal Cave, one of the scenic attractions in this area."

"Colossal Cave?" he echoed, a sneer in his voice. "I never heared of it."

"The Steffins family has a daughter by the name of Ingrid," Miss Duncan went on. "She's a little girl about twelve years old."

He ran his fingers through his shaggy hair.

"Steffins," he said, thinking hard. "Steffins. Seems as how I recollect somethin' about them. I think they did have a cave hereabouts. But it wasn't nothin' but a tourist trap, an' people soon wised up an' quit stoppin' there. They finally had to quit. Come to think of it, they did call their little hole in the ground 'Colossal Cave.' But it wasn't nothin' compared to what we've got."

He eyed them hopefully.

"If you got a few minutes to take the quick tour, ladies, you'll see the most wonderful sights you ever did see in all your borned lives. One of them Maharajahs from Guatemala or China, I forget which, was here year before last. He came back last year and brought his whole harem along just so they could see our cave."

Joan Bailey saw the lights go on in Miss Duncan's eyes the way they did when she was about to deal with an erring student.

"He'd better watch out," she snickered under her breath, "or he's going to catch it."

Instead, Miss Duncan went on coldly. "We're not interested in touring any caves at the moment."

"Not even at half price?"

She shook her head.

"Then what're you wastin' my time for?" He was about to turn and stomp back into the house.

"My good man, I have been trying to tell you that we would like to locate the Steffins family, and Ingrid in particular."

"Reckon that ain't goin' to be easy." He scratched his head again. "Pete Steffins pulled out when he couldn't make nothin' on his cave. Nobody round these parts has got any idee where he went." He shrugged his big shoulders. "And what's more, nobody cared a hoot. He was the biggest liar in these parts. You couldn't believe a word he said."

While they were talking, a pretty, dark-haired girl who faintly resembled the big man, came to the door of the little souvenir shop. She had been listening to the conversation.

"Uncle Dan," she said, "I know where–"

He froze her with a look.

"Betty, I reckon maybe you got somethin' to do inside. I'll talk to these here ladies."

The girl he had called Betty looked at Miss Duncan and Joan and Felicia longingly but did as she was told.

"Now, I reckon you'd better git on down the road if you don't want to buy nothin' or go through the cave. Women like you had oughta know better'n to waste honest folks' time."

CHAPTER 2

THE STEFFINS FAMILY

Miss Duncan got into the Volkswagen and backed up to turn out of the farmyard.

"That man!" she exploded.

"He certainly gave me the shivers," Joan Bailey put in. "Did you see the way he looked at us? Especially when you asked about the Steffins family."

"Apparently he has something against them," Felicia Cartright said. "He certainly doesn't care whether we locate them or not."

Miss Duncan pulled out onto the highway but drove considerably slower than before.

"A Wellington girl should not judge others at first meeting," she began. "Many jewels are thrown out with the wash water by such a procedure. But in the case of Daniel L. Julian, I believe we are safe in assuming that he is somewhat careless with the truth and not entirely to be trusted."

"That," Joan murmured beneath her breath, "is the understatement of the year."

"I think he knows where the Steffins family went, but he wouldn't tell us."

"I was thinking the same thing," Joan retorted. "Did you notice the way that girl looked at us? She acted as though she had something to tell us, but she was afraid to."

Felicia shuddered. "Can you blame her? I'd be afraid of him too."

It was a minute or two before Miss Duncan spoke again. "I wish it were possible for us to spend some time looking for the Steffins family. I would truly like to see Ingrid and talk with her. But I'm afraid we're going to have to go on to Springfield, since we're not at all sure they even live around here anymore."

"Don't you think she would have written you if they had moved?" Felicia asked.

"It would seem so. But I like to keep my trips on some sort of schedule, and we are not going to be able to do that if we linger here."

"They must live close," Joan said.

"If they are still in the area," Miss Duncan added.

"I can't understand why there are no signs along the highway advertising their cave," Felicia said thoughtfully. "It–" She checked herself suddenly. "Miss Duncan, stop!"

The driver slammed on the brakes, and the little Volkswagen skidded to a halt.

"What is it? What's wrong?"

"I saw something back there. I want to go back and see what it is."

"Felicia!" Miss Duncan exclaimed, her mouth drawn pencil-thin. "A Wellington girl is always poised and reserved. She is always considerate of others. When she wishes someone to do something for her, she always prefaces the request with 'please.' She doesn't yell like a–a banshee."

"Yes, Miss Duncan. I'm sorry, Miss Duncan."

Felicia opened the car door and ran back to a post she saw standing in the ditch. Miss Duncan backed up beside her.

The Cartright girl dashed into the ditch and picked up a board that was still attached to a second post. Several other boards were scattered about.

"Miss Duncan!" she cried. "Joan! Here's our sign!"

Her companions clambered out of the car and down into the ditch.

"So it is!" Miss Duncan exclaimed. "Colossal Cave 2 ½ miles." She took a deep breath. "The Steffins' farm must have been within half a mile or so of Daniel Julian and his Constellation Cave."

Joan's eyes flashed. "That Mr. Julian was so ornery and disagreeable he wouldn't have told us if they'd lived in the same house with him."

"Of course, the sign was down," Miss Duncan said. "That would be the logical procedure if the cave is no longer in operation."

"Maybe," Felicia said thoughtfully, "but if that was the case, wouldn't the signs have been taken down properly so they could have been used by someone else?"

For a long minute, Miss Duncan stood there, one of the broken boards from the sign in her hand. With her finger, she lightly rubbed an indentation left by the sledge or axe that had broken the sign.

"Are you thinking the same thing I'm thinking?" she asked at last.

"'Daniel L. Julian, Prop.'?" Felicia echoed.

"Exactly." Miss Duncan dropped the board and started back to the car. "But, no matter, we've got to be on our way if we're going to get to Springfield tonight."

Disappointment clouded the girls' faces.

"We're going back to see if the Steffins family is still there, aren't we?"

Miss Duncan hesitated. "I hadn't planned on it."

"It'll only take a few minutes," Joan Bailey put in. "If we don't, we'll never know whether that character at the other cave was telling us the truth or not."

"And," Felicia added significantly, "we won't get to see Ingrid."

Miss Duncan looked at her watch.

"I would like to see the girl," she said. "We'll note the time and get up enough earlier tomorrow morning to make up what we lose."

Joan Bailey groaned.

They checked the speedometer closely and drove back past Constellation Cave to the next farm a short distance beyond it. It was back from the road and all but obscured by trees.

"It's no wonder we didn't see it," Felicia said. "I saw the arrow, but there's no lettering on it that would indicate there's a tourist attraction here."

Miss Duncan downshifted as she pulled into the yard.

"Someone lives here, all right," she said. "There are curtains at the windows."

The house was a little bigger than the Julian place and better kept. It was fairly well painted and in good repair. The sign over the building that apparently housed the cave entrance was quite new.

"'Colossal Cave,'" Joan Bailey read. "This is the place, all right."

Even as she spoke, Felicia saw a kitchen curtain pull back and a small, flaxen head peer out.

"They still live here," she said quietly. "I'm sure I just saw Ingrid at the window."

Miss Duncan stopped.

"Why don't you go up to the door, Felicia? If this is the place, Joan and I can join you."

"And if it turns out to be another 'Daniel Julian, Prop.,'" Joan Bailey said, giggling, "we'll drive off and try to forget we ever knew you."

"You're a lot of help."

Felicia went up to the door and knocked.

All was silent inside.

She knocked again.

"Ingrid!" a man's tired voice called out. "Ingrid! Somebody's at the door!"

In the car, Miss Duncan and Joan waited tensely.

Felicia could hear reluctant footsteps cross the floor. The doorknob turned slowly, and a dark crack appeared between the edge of the door and the casing. Two small, frightened eyes peered out at her from an ashen face.

"Ingrid, who is it?"

"It's a lady, Paw!"

"Ask her what she wants."

The girl swallowed hard, and her thin voice was a squeak. "What do you want?"

Felicia smiled down at her reassuringly.

"Are you Ingrid?"

She nodded.

"I'm Miss Cartright from Wellington School for Girls."

Ingrid's eyes widened.

"And Miss Duncan is out in the car. You remember writing to her, don't you?"

Ingrid nodded wordlessly and opened the door wide enough for Felicia to come in. The Cartright girl stepped inside and looked around. Efforts had been made to keep the house clean, but the dishpan was full of dirty dishes, and the floor under the table and stove needed sweeping. The furnishings in the Steffins' home were sparse and meager.

"If you've come to sell something," a man said from the other room bitterly, "we don't want to buy it. If you've come to collect a bill, I haven't got any money. You'll have to wait."

"They're from that school I wrote to, Paw," Ingrid exclaimed, her eyes bright with excitement. "They stopped by to see me."

"I don't know what good it's going to do. We hardly have money enough to keep Ingrid in school now, let alone to send her away somewhere when she starts high school."

Felicia went to the door of the room where the voice was coming from and looked in.

"Oh, you're in bed. I'm sorry."

"I'm sorry, too." He laughed, but there was no mirth in his voice.

He was thin and pale, and his torso seemed to be in some sort of a cast.

"Broke my back a couple of months ago," he explained. "And things have been real tough around here ever since."

"That's too bad." She paused for an instant or two. "We don't want to bother you, Mr. Steffins, but Miss Duncan would like to see Ingrid if she may. She was so impressed with her letter."

"Suit yourself." Self-pity welled within him.

Ingrid turned to Felicia, her dark eyes dancing merrily.

"I knew you'd come," she exclaimed. "I just *knew* you'd come!"

Miss Duncan and Joan Bailey came into the house. Felicia introduced them to Mr. Steffins.

"I've got to apologize for the way the house looks," he said lamely. "Ingrid and Merle – he's my son – have been trying to keep things up the best they can, but it's been real hard for them with their mother dead."

"It hasn't been so hard for me since I became a Christian, Paw," the girl said quickly. "Jesus helps me in whatever I have to do."

The injured man's face hardened, and for an instant, anger glinted darkly in his eyes.

"How many times've I got to tell you not to talk that way, Ingrid?" he demanded. "There's nothing to the Bible or all that talk about salvation. If there is a God, He doesn't love us."

"Yes, He does, Mr. Steffins," Felicia said quietly. "He loves everybody."

The injured man glanced down at the cast that encased his torso. "If God loves us, He's sure got a funny way of showing it. That's all I can say."

Then, before anyone else could continue the subject, he started talking about something else.

Ingrid sat on a stool near her father's bed, looking at Miss Duncan in awe. As soon as she could manage, she began to ask questions about Wellington.

After a time, Felicia broke in. "There are some dirty dishes in the kitchen, Mr. Steffins," she said. "Joan and I will be glad to do them if you wouldn't be offended."

"Be offended?" he echoed. "I'd be right grateful to both of you."

Felicia and Joan did the dishes then swept the floor and straightened up the living room. They didn't realize how fast time was going until Miss Duncan came out into the kitchen.

"Are you girls about through?" she asked. "It's almost 6 o'clock."

"Six o'clock!" Joan exclaimed. "I had no idea!"

"I wish I was able to be up and around," Mr. Steffins said, gratitude coloring his voice. "I'd sure be proud to have you stay for supper. You know, that's the first time the dishes have all been washed in this house at the same time since before I went to the hospital with a broken back."

"Could they stay for supper, Paw?" Ingrid broke in. "Could they?"

"If they did, they'd have to cook it."

That seemed to settle the matter as far as Miss Duncan was concerned. She turned to the girls.

"If it's all right with Felicia and Joan," she said, "I find it agreeable."

The evening meal was almost ready when Merle Steffins came in. His dad introduced him to Felicia and Joan and Miss Duncan.

"They're from the school where Mrs. Porter went," Mr. Steffins explained. "Ingrid wrote to Miss Duncan, and since they were going by, they decided to stop and see her."

"Oh." Disappointment showed on the boy's tanned young face. "I was hoping we had some people to go through the cave." He went over and sat down wearily. "I just can't figure it out. We haven't had anybody stopping the last few days."

"Maybe there aren't as many tourists."

"That's not it, Paw." He sighed wearily. "There are more cars on the road than ever."

"We had quite a time finding your place," Felicia Cartright told them. "We didn't see any signs and–"

"Didn't see any signs?" Merle broke in. "You should've. We've got signs up and down the highway for twenty-five miles or so. I know. I put them up myself."

Miss Duncan came to the bedroom door.

"Just the same, young man, your signs are not up now. If you'll go down the road two or three miles, you'll find that your sign has been taken down, broken in pieces, and is lying in the ditch."

Merle Steffins' face darkened.

"That does it, Paw! That does it!" He got up and paced across the room and back. Ever since old Daniel Julian opened up his Constellation Cave, we've had nothing but trouble."

"We've got no call to blame Julian, Merle. We don't know that he did it."

"Who else would do a thing like that?" His voice was taut and high-pitched. "I tell you, Paw, he's caused us all the trouble he's goin' to. I'm going over and have it out with him."

Mr. Steffins' anger flared.

"You're not doing anything of the kind. We've got enough trouble without havin' you go over there and make things worse. You just sit down and cool yourself off, boy. We're goin' to have supper in a little while."

"We stopped at Constellation Cave," Joan began, "and Daniel Julian told us that–"

"Miss Bailey," Miss Duncan broke in suddenly, "I think we need a chair from the barn."

"I just got one." Joan protested.

"We need another one."

Merle got to his feet. "I'll get it for you."

As soon as Merle was out of the house on his way to the barn, Mr. Steffins turned to Miss Duncan.

"Thank you, lady. That boy's so hot-headed I've had one terrible time holding him down. It doesn't do any good to give that kind of tale to him."

Miss Duncan nodded in agreement, then directed her attention to Joan Bailey.

"Now, I think it would be wise to tell Mr. Steffins what you were about to say."

"I–I was just going to tell you that Mr. Julian wouldn't even direct us to your place. He said that you had—had gone broke and moved away and nobody knew where."

The injured man's eyes narrowed to slits.

"The going broke part's about nine-tenths right, but we haven't run away yet. And we're not going to if I can help it."

Merle came back just then, and they changed the subject quickly.

"I think dinner is ready now," Miss Duncan said.

They pushed Mr. Steffins' hospital bed to the bedroom door so he could see and cranked it up slightly. He frowned a little when Miss Duncan asked for permission to have Felicia ask the blessing.

"I guess no harm can come from it," he muttered, "nor much good either."

Felicia saw the hurt leap to Ingrid's youthful eyes.

When they finished eating, Felicia and Joan got to work clearing the table and washing the dishes.

Mr. Steffins looked around. "This kitchen hasn't been so clean since my wife died," he said gratefully.

"It must be difficult for two men and a girl the age of Ingrid to keep things up properly," Miss Duncan said.

He drew a deep breath.

"I know I haven't got any call to ask you this, but we sure would appreciate it if you could stick around for a day or two."

Ingrid's whole face lit up.

"Oh, do!"

"We've got plenty of room for you," the older man went on. "It isn't so nice, but it's clean."

For a moment or two Miss Duncan surveyed the situation. "Thank you," she said. "We'll stay the night, at least."

When they were alone in their room, Felicia and Joan turned quickly to her.

"If we could stay for a couple of days to help Ingrid get the house completely cleaned once, it would be much easier for her," Felicia said.

"We could do the washing and the ironing," Joan put in, "and maybe do some baking so they would have some pies and cakes to eat for a change."

Miss Duncan surveyed them knowingly.

"I don't suppose that handsome older brother has a thing to do with all of this."

Joan Bailey flushed.

"What makes you say that?"

The dean of Wellington smiled. "I haven't been around girls for twenty years without learning something."

CHAPTER 3

COLOSSAL CAVE

The following morning, Miss Duncan and the girls were up an hour before they usually were and had the teakettle singing on the stove and the table set before any of the Steffins family appeared.

"Well," Miss Duncan said in a tone that made it difficult to tell whether she was teasing or not, "have you girls decided which is to get the handsome young man we're staying to help?"

Felicia laughed, and twin spots of color delicately stained her cheeks.

"Not yet."

Joan Bailey did the same.

"It seems quite unfortunate to me," Miss Duncan went on, her expression not changing, "that two upstanding young Wellington girls would stoop to the deception of staying here to help a little sister when there's another motive, more foul, behind it."

"Deception?" they echoed. "What do you mean?"

"Now, don't try to be so innocent. You forget that I've been dealing with girls like you since before you were born." Miss Duncan laughed musically. "I know you want to stay here because you're after Merle Steffins. You can't deceive me."

"We didn't know it showed," Felicia said.

Joan Bailey giggled. "You know, Miss Duncan, Felicia's so good with housework that I thought I'd leave that to her. I'll go out and help Merle paint new road signs and put them up."

Miss Duncan's lips straightened. "You'll do nothing of the kind. You will stay right here in the kitchen and help Felicia and me. If I am going to referee this–this affair, I'm going to see that no one has an undue advantage."

A moment later, Ingrid stole quietly into the kitchen, her shoes in her hand.

"Good morning," the girls said cheerfully.

"Hello." She sat down on a chair and looked at Felicia and Joan somberly. "If you were talking about Merle," she went on, "he doesn't like girls yet."

Felicia and Joan almost choked. "W–were you listening to us just now?"

"A–a little."

"You won't say anything to him about this, will you, Ingrid?" Felicia pleaded seriously.

She shook her head. "Not if you don't want me to."

"We don't want you to." Joan exclaimed. "Believe me."

For a couple of minutes, nobody said anything.

"I–I prayed and prayed that you would stay with us for a few days," Ingrid said finally. "You're going to, aren't you?"

Miss Duncan flashed her a quick smile. "Would you like that?"

"Oh, yes!" Her eyes danced. "That would be so very nice."

"It certainly would," Mr. Steffins called from the bedroom.

After breakfast, Merle went out to the barn to work on some new road signs.

"I've got to get them up right away to let people know our place is here. Fortunately, I already had a couple built and about half painted. I was going to put them up on the other side of Lodgeville."

The girls got to work in the house, clearing the breakfast dishes and washing them. Once that was accomplished, they began in the living room to give the house a thorough cleaning. They took down the pictures, cleaned the walls and ceiling, and washed the woodwork. Ingrid stayed beside them doing what she could and chattering constantly.

It was the middle of the morning when Felicia went out to get another bucket from the barn. Merle Steffins saw her and came over quickly.

"Here, let me do that for you."

"I can manage."

"Not when I'm around," he told her firmly.

He was a handsome young man, she had to agree. He was slender and broad-shouldered with a clean, square cut face and hair as dark as Ingrid's was light.

"How are the signs coming?" Felicia asked.

"I've got them right out here behind the barn." He set down the bucket. "Come and have a look."

She glanced back toward the house. "They're probably waiting for this."

"They'll be glad for a little breather." He started behind the barn, and she hurried to catch up with him. "I think I'll be able to finish them today," he told her. "In the morning, I'll load them in the pickup and put them up."

Merle had moved the signs out of the barn and had been working with them propped against the building.

"They do look nice," Felicia said.

"And if that Daniel Julian tears these down again, he'll have to answer to me." His fists clenched until his knuckles showed white, and his dark eyes flashed. "I'm going to get even with him yet."

Felicia Cartright frowned. "It bothers me to hear you talk that way. You sound so–so vengeful."

"Believe me, I am vengeful! If I could get my hands on that character, I'd break him in two."

"The Bible tells us that punishing others is for the law or God to do. We're not to take it on ourselves."

He straightened and looked at her curiously.

"You act as though you're a smart girl. Do you honestly believe all that stuff?"

"All of what stuff?" she asked him.

"All that stuff in the Bible," he went on. "The stuff Ingrid comes home and tries to tell Dad and me."

"I believe that the Bible is the Word of God," Felicia Cartright said simply. "I believe what the Bible says about man being a sinner and deserving to go to hell. I believe that the only way we can be saved is to confess our sin and put our trust in Jesus Christ for salvation."

Merle's face was hard. "You believe what you want to, and I'll believe what I want to." He turned and walked thoughtfully back toward the house.

When Merle and Felicia entered the house, Joan Bailey looked up.

"Cheater."

Felicia flushed.

"What was that?" the boy asked.

"It's just a personal matter," the Bailey girl told him.

While Felicia and Joan finished the living room and Ingrid's bedroom, Miss Duncan baked pies and a couple of cakes. That evening they sat down to a big meal.

"We haven't eaten like this around here for a long while," Mr. Steffins said. "And it's going to be so good to have the house completely cleaned again. It'll seem more like living around here, won't it, kids?"

"I am very proud of our Wellington girls," Miss Duncan said. "They have demonstrated that they are equal to any emergency and are very capable in a household."

The following day, the girls finished cleaning the rest of the house and were ready to leave, but the Steffins family prevailed on them to stay.

"There isn't any call to get out on the highway on the weekend," Peter Steffin said. "Why don't you stay with us until Monday morning?"

"Besides," Merle put in, "we haven't had a chance to show you the cave yet. You can't leave without seeing the most beautiful cave in Missouri."

Felicia and Joan looked to Miss Duncan hopefully. The older woman pursed her lips.

"We should be moving on," she said, "but I don't like to make it a practice of traveling on the Lord's Day."

"Then you'll stay with us," the injured man said, as though that decided it.

"Do stay!" Ingrid exclaimed. "Then you can go to church with me. And maybe Merle will go too."

His face colored deeply, and he looked down. "I don't think you'd better count on me," he said. "I've got somethin' to do tomorrow morning."

As soon as they finished eating lunch, Mr. Steffins insisted that they go down into the cave with Merle.

"I want you to see what we've got here," he said. "We really believe our advertising slogan, that we have one of the finest scenic attractions in the Ozarks. And I think you will agree with me when you see our cave."

They went out to the entrance, and Merle started the small generator that lit the cave.

"In case you're wondering," he said lamely, "the plant isn't big enough to supply lights for the house and the cave both. And besides, it takes money for wiring." There was bitterness in his voice.

They went down a series of steps in the first tunnel to a small grotto-like chamber with a forest of stalactites spiking the roof, like a million dripless icicles. Stalagmites sprouted here and there, spidery sentinels in the silent half-darkness of the dimly lit room.

"Listen," Felicia said, her voice soft and small, "you can almost *hear* the silence."

"I never heard anyone say it that way," Merle told her, "but I've often thought that when I've been down here alone."

They went through another small passageway and into a second room. There the lights were so arranged as to bring out the delicate coloring of the formations.

"We don't say this when we're showing tourists through," Merle said, "but we have only clear lights in here. We could make the colors much sharper by using colored bulbs. And we don't have anything to say against those who do, but Paw wants people to see the cave as it really is and to appreciate its true beauty." He took a long breath. "So, we're not such terrible monsters as you seem to think."

"But we don't think you're monsters," Felicia countered. "Whatever gave you that idea?"

"You said so yourself yesterday morning. You said we were so bad that we couldn't go to heaven unless we became Christians like you and Ingrid."

"I didn't say that," the girl answered. "If I did, it wouldn't have made any difference. What I say doesn't count for anything. The thing that counts is what the Bible says because it's the Word of God. And the Bible says that all have sinned and come short of the glory of God and that the wages of sin is death."

The defiance seemed to leave Merle's taut face. He took them on into the next chamber in the cave. From that moment on, the tour became cold and impersonal. They were getting the tourist lecture without warmth and friendliness. For the rest of the day, Merle Steffin was very quiet.

That afternoon, while Merle went out to put up his signs, Ingrid got into the front seat of the Volkswagen and guided the girls and Miss Duncan on a tour of the surrounding area.

"Dad says that there are higher mountains here in America," she said, "but that there aren't any that are any prettier." There was pride in her voice.

"It's beautiful," Miss Duncan answered.

After a time, Felicia asked Ingrid about the girl over at Constellation Cave.

"Oh, yes," she answered, "everybody knows Betty. She's sweet." Her face lit up. "She's my Sunday school teacher."

"That's interesting."

"I guess that's why I like Betty so much – next to Mrs. Porter. They were the ones who talked to me about the Lord and – helped me to become a Christian." Her face grew serious. "Only don't say anything to Paw about it. About Betty teaching my Sunday school class, I mean."

"Why not?" Miss Duncan wanted to know.

"I'm afraid he wouldn't let me go to Sunday school if he knew Betty was my teacher. He's awful mad at Mr. Julian, and he won't believe that Betty isn't like her uncle at all."

"You won't have to worry. We won't tell him."

The following morning, they went to church with Ingrid in the white Volkswagen. As soon as they came up to the front steps, Betty Julian came over to them.

"You're the girls who stopped at our place the other day, aren't you?" she asked.

"That's right."

"I'm so glad you found the Steffins place. I was going to come out and tell you, but my uncle–"

Felicia's smile was warm and friendly. "We know."

"He would have been terribly angry if I'd said anything to you." Her voice lowered. "I'm so glad you came to help the Steffins family. It's been so hard for them since Mr. Steffins got hurt."

Before the Cartright girl could reply, another car stopped before the little church. Betty looked up. Embarrassment stained her cheeks.

"I'm sorry," she muttered. "I've got to run."

"Now what's the matter with her?" Joan Bailey wondered aloud.

"She acts that way with Merle, too," Ingrid said. "She'll talk real nice to him as long as nobody else is around. I–I think she's afraid her Uncle Dan will find out about it."

Felicia Cartright's eyes filled with compassion. "That poor girl. She must be terribly afraid of him."

CHAPTER 4

DISABLED VOLKSWAGEN

Felicia Cartright was strangely quiet the rest of the afternoon. Miss Duncan noticed it and called her aside.

"Felicia," she said firmly, "there's something wrong with you."

The Cartright girl eyed her blankly. "There isn't anything wrong, Miss Duncan."

"Do you feel all right?"

"I feel fine."

The dean's eyes narrowed suspiciously.

"You aren't taking that young man too seriously, are you?"

"Of course not!" She was horrified at the thought.

"Then what is the matter with you?"

"Nothing. Nothing at all, except that I feel bad about having to leave the Steffins family when they need help so badly."

Miss Duncan nodded in agreement. "Quite true. And most commendable, but we must go on."

"At least," Felicia added, "we have the satisfaction of knowing that the house is clean and they have some things baked to eat."

"And," Miss Duncan went on, "I think Ingrid has learned a few simple skills during the course of our stay here."

* * *

Monday morning Miss Duncan and the girls set their alarm for 5:00 a.m. and got up in the chill darkness and dressed. However, Ingrid and Merle were already sitting in the kitchen waiting for them when they came down for breakfast. Ingrid was wearing her saddest face.

"Do you have to go?" she asked sorrowfully.

"I'm afraid so," Felicia answered.

"We're sure going to miss you," Merle said.

Miss Duncan smiled archly.

"You don't know how good it is to get the kind of meals you've been fixing for us."

"Oh," Miss Duncan said. "That's what you had reference to."

Joan and Felicia half turned away to keep him from seeing the color in their cheeks.

"The kids aren't the only ones who are going to

miss you," Mr. Steffins said from his bedroom. "Not that Ingrid doesn't do the best she can!"

While the girls took their luggage to the car reluctantly, Miss Duncan fixed breakfast. Nobody spoke much during the meal.

When they finished eating, Ingrid got up suddenly and went in to whisper to her dad. Then she went outside, and in a couple of minutes, returned carrying her puppy, Southern Gentleman, better known as "Nosy."

Joan Bailey stroked the pup tenderly. "Good old Nosy."

A smile flashed across Ingrid's face and came to rest in her eyes.

"I'm giving him to you." She placed Nosy in Joan's lap. "I talked with Daddy about it, and he said I could."

"But Ingrid!" Felicia exclaimed, "you don't want to give us your dog."

"Oh, but I do. You've done so much good for us and–" Her voice was so shaky that she could not speak immediately. "That is–that is if you want him."

"Want him?" Joan Bailey exclaimed. "He's about the most beautiful dog I've ever seen."

Felicia put her arm around Ingrid and hugged her tightly.

"We can never thank you girls enough," Mr. Steffins put in. "You've given us a new interest in life, coming in and giving us a hand this way."

"We can keep Nosy in the dorm next year, can't we, Miss Duncan?" the Bailey girl asked.

"Well," she said frowning, "that is something we will have to see about later on." She looked down at her watch. "It's after six. We must be leaving."

But when they got into the Volkswagen and she tried to start it, nothing happened.

"That's strange," she murmured. "It worked fine yesterday when we drove to church." She tried again, but the engine didn't start.

Merle Steffins, who was standing on the back porch watching, came out to the car.

"It's not turning over."

Miss Duncan got out of the car, strode to the back purposefully, and opened the lid on the engine compartment. Only then did she straighten uncertainly and turn to Merle.

"Young man, do you know anything about the innards of this engine?"

He shook his head.

"You do, too, Merle," Ingrid broke in. "You've worked on our pickup lots of times."

He flushed slightly. "Sure," he acknowledged, "but this is a foreign car and I–I just don't know anything about them. The only thing I know is to get to town and get a mechanic to come out and fix it."

Miss Duncan pushed a strand of hair back in place. "There's no reception out here, so may I use your home phone to contact a mechanic and get him out here to take a look at this?"

"Our phone's not in working order. Something happened to our line a couple of weeks ago, and it hasn't been fixed yet."

"I see." She thought for an instant. "May we borrow your truck to drive to Lodgeville and find a garage?" Merle eyed her uncertainly.

"We'd be glad to loan the pickup to you, of course," he said with reluctance, "but the mechanics at Lodgeville are real funny. If they don't know you, I don't think they'd even come out to fix it."

"Perhaps we could tow it to town," Felicia suggested.

"Oh, I think I know a man who'd come out for me," Merle said quickly, "only I'd have to go in town myself and see him. It wouldn't do any good for you to go."

He started for the house.

"I'll change clothes and go to town for you."

"I don't like to put you to that trouble, Merle," Miss Duncan told him.

"After what you've done for us?"

He was ready to get into his pickup to go to Lodgeville for a mechanic when a carload of tourists came up. He went over to their car and, in a moment or two, took them down to the cave.

"It looks as though you have some customers, Mr. Steffins," Miss Duncan said from the window.

"Those signs Merle put up must be doing a little

good." The very fact that they were again attracting customers seemed to materially affect his spirits. "Merle will go to town to see about getting a mechanic out here as soon as these people leave."

"That's quite all right. We're enjoying our stay here."

Mr. Steffins eyed her strangely, and his lips parted as though to speak, but he changed his mind and said nothing.

Miss Duncan went to the window again as the car of visitors drove away. They were not out of the yard, however, before a second car pulled in. And so went the morning.

Merle only had time to step in and snatch a bite to eat.

"You aren't going to be able to go to town, Merle, if this keeps up," his dad said. "Don't you think it would be better if the girls took our truck and went into Lodgeville to get someone to repair their car? Much as we'd like to have them stay, we can't delay them any longer."

The boy's eyes flashed. "You know old Charlie, Paw. The chances are he wouldn't even come out for them."

"There's another mechanic in town."

"But he's hardly got any tools or anything. And besides, he's there all alone. He couldn't leave his shop."

"Don't worry about us, Mr. Steffins," Miss Duncan put in. "Our stay here must be ordered of the Lord. We won't question it."

Merle Steffins flinched, and a line around his lips grew white. Felicia thought she saw his hand tremble as he picked up his coffee and gulped it.

"I'd better get goin'," he said. "Those last people told me there were two other cars just behind them that were going to stop here. I sure don't want to miss 'em." At the door, he paused and turned back. "I'll sure be able to get in town this afternoon."

"That will be fine, Merle," Miss Duncan said calmly. "Ingrid and I have some special plans for this afternoon."

"Miss Duncan's going to tell me all about the school," his younger sister exclaimed, eyes dancing. "And I'm going to take her up on the mountain and show her the flowers."

Felicia Cartright and Joan Bailey finished the dishes and straightened up the kitchen.

Merle's customers did show up before long, and there was every evidence that he would be busy most of the afternoon.

Felicia and Joan went out on the back porch.

"It seems strange to me," Joan said, "that we couldn't tow Miss Duncan's car to Lodgeville or get a mechanic out here ourselves to get it fixed."

"You know how some people are," Felicia countered. "Perhaps this Charlie doesn't know or trust strangers."

Joan giggled. "Maybe Merle doesn't want to get

a mechanic out here because he doesn't want you to leave."

"Why me? He talks to you as much as he does to me. More, probably."

"But he doesn't have that twinkle in his eye." Joan Bailey sauntered down the steps and out to the car. "Know what? I'll bet Miss Duncan is already saying to herself, 'A Wellington girl must be prepared to meet any eventuality.' And she's undoubtedly working out a short course in mechanics for us."

"This is delaying us," Felicia continued, "but it might give us another opportunity to speak to them about the Lord."

Joan Bailey nodded. "The trouble is that they're such nice people they feel they don't need Christ as their Savior. Mr. Steffins is kind and honest, and he's really good to his family."

"If they could just see that that isn't enough," Felicia said, "that no matter how good they are, they can never be good enough to merit salvation."

They went out to the car and stood for a moment or two looking at it.

"It isn't like Miss Duncan to have something go wrong," Joan said. "She's so careful to have everything in perfect working order before she does anything."

Felicia walked around to the other side.

"I didn't think Miss Duncan had any tools out here this morning," she said, stooping to pick up a screwdriver that was lying just behind the back wheel.

"She didn't."

Joan took the screwdriver and examined it curiously.

"Maybe it was here when we drove up," she said.

"It couldn't have been. It was lying right behind the rear wheel, and we hadn't run over it."

"That's strange." The Bailey girl turned it in her hand. "It wouldn't be Miss Duncan's. It says, 'Made in USA.' Her tools would have come from Germany."

Felicia's mouth tightened, and there was a glint in her eyes as she put the screwdriver into her jacket pocket.

"She only raised the lid and looked at the engine. She didn't have a tool in her hand."

"Maybe it's Merle's."

"He didn't look at the engine either, remember? He said he didn't know anything about foreign cars."

"Where did it come from then?" Joan wanted to know.

Felicia shook her head. "All I know is that our car won't run, and somebody lost a screwdriver behind it."

They walked a few paces up the lane.

"You don't suppose somebody deliberately did something to Miss Duncan's car, do you?" Joan asked.

"There's only one person I know around here who would do a thing like that."

"Daniel Julian?"

"And I can't figure out why he would. We sure haven't done anything to him."

"No, and there's nothing he could gain by keeping us here," Joan added.

Joan Bailey picked up a stick and tossed it to one side.

"Unless he *thinks* there's something he could gain by keeping us here."

Joan laughed. "You're going to have to spell it out to me, Felicia. You don't come through at all when you talk like that."

"I don't have anything in mind, really. I was just thinking out loud. We have good reason to believe that he broke up the signs Mr. Steffins had up advertising the cave. He might figure there's some way he can hurt the Colossal Cave as a tourist attraction by keeping us around."

"I don't get it."

"Neither do I. Just skip it."

They walked to the end of the lane and along the highway slowly. A scant hundred yards beyond the turnoff to the Steffins' farm and Colossal Cave, Felicia paused.

"That's strange," she murmured.

"Now what's bothering you?"

"Somebody went off the road with a big truck or something. They went down this ditch and up the other side. You can see the tracks as plain as day."

"Maybe they've got a field up there," Joan said.

"No. There's no farming up the mountain beyond the Steffins' place. I heard Mr. Steffins tell Miss

Duncan that when they were talking last night." Joan shrugged. "But I don't suppose that means anything either."

"I don't know for sure," her companion replied. "Daniel Julian could have used those trees as a screen to get up close to the house so he could come over and sabotage our car."

Joan laughed. "Now that is something. Driving a noisy old tractor over to an enemy's house so he could sneak up and knock out the engine of Miss Duncan's car."

"I guess that isn't so logical when you put it that way."

"No, but it makes awfully good detective material."

Felicia went down into the ditch and examined the tracks carefully.

"I'll admit it sounds crazy," she said, "but these tracks are fresh. They almost look as though they were made this morning."

"They couldn't have been made this morning. We'd have seen a tractor go by the house if we'd been up. And if we hadn't seen it, we'd have heard it."

A strange look came into Felicia's eyes. "Why would anyone drive a tractor up a mountainside at night?"

"I don't know, but we can follow it and find out."

CHAPTER 5

MYSTERIOUS TRACKS

Joan Bailey and Felicia Cartright followed the tractor tracks up the mountain.

"I hope nobody sees us and asks what we're doing," Felicia said. "I'd feel awfully silly having to tell them."

Joan giggled infectiously. "They'd probably just say that they couldn't expect any more out of a couple of stupid tourists."

The tractor tracks followed the fence line for a hundred yards or so, angled across a shallow gully, and continued to climb.

"We didn't see any footprints leading to our car," Joan said, "so whoever came up here must not have had anything to do with our car refusing to run."

Felicia, who was several steps ahead of Joan, stopped abruptly at the edge of a shallow mountain stream.

"Now what?" Joan Bailey asked, moving up beside her.

"The tracks disappear right here at the water's edge."

"They don't come out the other side either."

They took off their shoes and socks and walked across the shallow creek.

"There's rock on this side," Felicia Cartright said after a time. "I don't believe they'd leave any tracks over here."

They searched the entire area carefully, but there was no sign that the tractor had moved an inch beyond the water's edge.

"Isn't that strange?" Felicia murmured.

"I know what happened," Joan said. "Someone flew down in his helicopter, hooked on the tractor, and whisked it away."

"Silly."

"You give me a better explanation of what happened."

Felicia stood erect.

"I suppose we'd just as well give up on this. It's getting late. Miss Duncan will be wondering where we've been."

They started back to the Steffins' farm.

"Are we going to say anything to Miss Duncan about this?" Felicia wondered.

"Are you kidding? She thinks we're scatterbrained enough already. If we tell her what we've been doing this afternoon, she'll be sure we need a psychiatrist or a stay in some nice, quiet institution."

"I suppose you're right."

They walked on in silence until they reached the road.

Shading her eyes, Felicia stared in the direction of Constellation Cave. "I still would like to know if the tractor we've been trying to follow came from Dan Julian's."

"They did enter the ditch from that direction."

Felicia lowered her voice as though Julian could somehow hear every word that was said. "I think we ought to pay a visit to Mr. Julian and see if we can find out what kind of a tractor he's got."

Joan Bailey shuddered. "There you go again. I might've known you'd be wanting to get back over there. You're going to be the death of me yet."

When they got back to the Steffins' house a few minutes before dinner, Merle had just returned from town.

"I had quite a time talking Charlie into it," he said. "But he finally agreed to come out and take a look at the Volkswagen."

"When can we expect him?" Mr. Steffins asked.

"Paw!" Exasperation kindled in Merle's face. "You've known Charlie since before I was born. You know you don't get much out of him. He didn't even want to come and work on a foreign car at all, but he did say he'd do it."

"Did you talk to that new guy like I told you to?"

"I saw him. He's the most independent character

you ever did see. He said he wouldn't even fix it if we towed it into his shop and lifted the lid for him."

Mr. Steffins sighed deeply. "I guess that's all you could do then. I hate to hold the girls up any longer than absolutely necessary. They've been such a help to us already. We can't impose on them."

The next morning, the girls got up early and got to work fixing breakfast.

"You girls don't have to do that," Mr. Steffins said.

"As long as we're here, we might as well," Felicia told him.

For a brief space of time, he was quiet.

"It was certainly our lucky day when you girls stopped by here," he said finally, as though he had been thinking about it for a long while. "I don't know what we'd have done without you."

"Miss Duncan says she doesn't think it was chance that caused Ingrid to write to the school or luck that caused us to stop here. She feels that God sent us here in answer to Ingrid's prayers."

The gratitude fled from Mr. Steffins' face. The lights in his eyes dimmed, and the muscles around his mouth tightened.

"You call it what you want to," he said coldly, "and I'll call it what I want to."

Felicia went to the door and saw that there was nothing for her to do for a few minutes.

"You feel the way you do, Mr. Steffins," she said, "because you've never trusted Christ as your Savior."

Bitterness edged his voice. "God's never done anything for me."

"Oh, yes He has," she replied quickly.

"You talk that way because you don't know. You've never had to face the problems I've had to face." His voice grew louder as he continued to talk. "Just take a look at me, Felicia. Here I am lying flat on my back and not able to do a thing. My wife died, and I'm left with a pile of bills and two kids to support. You can't tell me that if there is a God He knows or cares anything about Peter Steffins."

Felicia paused for a moment, hunting for words.

"I certainly haven't had the problems you've had, Mr. Steffins," she said. "That's true. And I can't begin to tell why they would all happen to you when someone else like Dan Julian would have no serious trials – at least that we know about. But this much I do know. God loved you so much He sent His Son, Jesus Christ, to die on the cross so you could be saved."

Hurt flickered in his eyes. He closed them quickly and, for a time, breathed heavily. While Felicia prayed for guidance, Miss Duncan, Merle, and Ingrid came down into the kitchen.

"Well," Miss Duncan said approvingly, "you girls are proceeding very well."

"You can say that again," the injured man replied. "I think the fortunes of the Steffins family are going to change now. In fact, I know our fortunes are going to change when I find that new cave."

Felicia turned to him. "Do you think there's another cave on this farm?" she asked incredulously.

"I know there is. My grandfather used to tell me about it when I was a boy. He found it as a young man and did quite a bit of exploring. He said it was bigger than any of the other caves in these parts and was so much more beautiful than the others that they couldn't begin to compare with it."

"Didn't he tell you where it was?"

"That's the trouble. He told us all about it, but he would never tell us where it was. He said it was too dangerous for anyone to go into, so he kept it a secret."

Miss Duncan, who had one ear tuned to the conversation, came to the bedroom door. "He must have been a very thoughtful man."

"You can say that again. Granddad was thoughtful, and he was good. Everybody in these parts spoke well of him." He eyed them obliquely. "And he didn't go for all this religious stuff either."

"How sad."

Mr. Steffins bristled. "Now you're not going to try to tell me that a man who was as good and kind as my granddad wouldn't go to heaven, are you?"

"The Bible says, *But we are all as an unclean thing*," Miss Duncan quoted quietly, "*and all our righteousnesses are as filthy rags; and we all do fade as a leaf; and our iniquities, like the wind, have taken us away.*"

"But he was a good man."

"The Word of God tells us that there isn't any

such thing," Miss Duncan went on. "And there are no good women either. No one but Christ has lived a perfect life. And only one who is perfect can stand before God."

His face drained of color.

"That's a harsh statement, Miss Duncan," he said lamely, "and a little hard on those of us who try to live the best we can – isn't it?"

"You and I might wish that it be different," she told him. "We might even deceive ourselves into thinking that it is different. But that won't change things at all. God's Word is very clear, and nothing we can say or do can change it."

His thin mouth twitched.

"If a person can't be good enough to go to heaven, how can he get there?"

Merle stood immediately.

"Paw," he broke in, "I think breakfast is about ready."

"You asked me a question," Miss Duncan said calmly, ignoring the interruption. "We can't get to heaven by being good enough. The Bible says so, and the Bible is the Word of God. But God knows all about our sin. He knows that we are all sinners and the wages of sin is death. Yet He loved us so very much that He sent His only Son to die on the cross and be raised again so that we can be saved and go to heaven."

"I don't understand it."

"I don't understand it either," Miss Duncan told him. "I'm not sure that anyone does. But the Bible says that if we confess our sin and put our trust in Him, He will save us. And I know it works because I've done it."

He turned the matter over in his mind. "Is that the reason you and the girls are different than most other people we know?"

"If we're different, that's the reason."

"It's something to think about," he said, measuring the words. "It's something to think about."

Breakfast was ready, and there was no opportunity for Miss Duncan to continue the conversation further.

When they had finished eating and the dishes and housework were done, Felicia and Joan told Miss Duncan they were going for a walk.

"I'd like to go along," she said, "but I suppose I had better stay here in case the mechanic comes out from Lodgeville."

"May I go?" Ingrid asked.

Felicia Cartright hesitated. "We might be walking quite far."

"Oh, that's all right," the girl exclaimed. "I'm never too tired to go for a walk."

"I suppose it will be all right," Felicia answered, trying to keep her reluctance from showing through.

"Oh, thank you!" She ran to get the old slouch hat that had belonged to Merle. In a minute, she was back. "Nosy can go along, too, can't he?"

"I think so," Joan replied. "Nosy's going to have to start getting used to us if he's going to be our dog."

"You're going to love him. I know you will."

"We love him already." Joan stopped and bent to pet the long-eared puppy.

The three girls sauntered aimlessly down the lane.

"Where're we going?" Ingrid asked pointedly.

"For a walk," Felicia answered.

"Are we going over to Mr. Julian's cave?" As she spoke her voice dropped to a whisper.

"What makes you think that?" Joan asked.

"Are we?"

Felicia and Joan glanced at one another questioningly.

"Ingrid," Felicia began, putting her arm around their twelve-year-old companion, "can you keep a secret?"

Their eyes met.

"I didn't tell anybody that you picked up a screwdriver behind your car."

"How did you know about that?"

"I saw you pick up something and talk for a little while, standing real close together. Then you put it in your jacket pocket."

"But how did you know it was a screwdriver?"

"When you weren't looking, I peeked." Her eyes grew even more serious. "But I didn't say anything to anyone about it. Honestly, I didn't. Cross my heart."

"We were sure you could keep a secret," Felicia

told her. "That's why we agreed to take you along. If you won't tell anyone unless they ask you straight out – we wouldn't want you to lie – we'll tell you where we're going and why."

Ingrid listened wide-eyed as Joan and Felicia explained the purpose of their visit to the Julian place.

"But don't *ever* let him know why we're there," Joan whispered fearfully. "He'd get *awful* mad."

It was only a little more than a mile to the Julian cave, and they walked it in about twenty minutes. Dan Julian was nowhere to be seen, but Betty was in the souvenir shop. As soon as they entered, she came up to them.

"Hello." Her smile was warm and friendly. "I didn't know you were still around."

"We wouldn't have been, but we had car trouble," the girls explained.

"Oh, that's too bad."

Silence hung between them.

"Is–is your uncle around?" Joan asked. She tried hard to sound casual, but it didn't come off very well.

"There he is now." Her manner seemed to turn to ice as she watched Dan Julian guide a carload of tourists toward the souvenir shop. "Oh, he's coming in here!" She reached for something on the counter and knocked off a pile of pennants and key chains.

Mr. Julian came into the souvenir shop and held the door open for his visitors.

"I just want you to see the finest bunch of junk

– I mean collection of items you'll find in any of the souvenir shops from here to either coast," he blustered. "Only the best is good enough for Dan'l Julian. Ain't that right, Betty?"

She did not answer him.

"Ain't that right, Betty?" His voice rose and had an edge.

"You have *some* nice things, Uncle Dan," she mumbled.

Dan Julian gave no indication that he recognized Felicia and Joan when they were in the shop. But the instant they stepped outside, he pounced on them.

"What're you doin' here?"

"We walked down from the Steffins' place," Joan said evenly.

"I *got* eyes!" he roared. "I know you walked down from the Steffins' place. What I want to know is, how come you're still hangin' around these parts? And what're you doin' snoopin' around over here?"

Nobody spoke.

"You!" He directed his wrath toward Ingrid. "What're they doin' over here?"

Fear leaped to her eyes, but she didn't say a word.

"You know what they're doin' here, don't you?" He grasped her arm and started to squeeze it.

"Mr. Julian!" Felicia cried, her face white with rage. "You take your hands off her!"

"Then s'posin' you tell me what this's all about?" He relaxed his grip ever so slightly.

Felicia swallowed against the lump in her throat. "Somebody was driving a tractor up the mountain near the Steffins' home," she blurted, "and we came over to see if you had a tractor that made a track like the one we saw there."

"I suppose Pete sent you!"

"He had nothing to do with it. And neither did Merle."

"Don't give me that stuff!" His voice snarled. "I know that character well enough to know better."

"We're telling you the truth," Felicia said, "whether you believe it or not."

"I don't believe it," he retorted, "but just in case you've still got any more stupid ideas about me drivin' a tractor up the mountain near Pete Steffins, I want you to come out here with me."

He started for the barn, still holding Ingrid lightly by the arm. "I want you to see my tractor. You can make up your own mind whether I've got a tractor that would make tracks like you saw – or thought you saw."

He jerked open the barn door to reveal a small tractor with tires half the size of those that had made the marks in the ditch and up to the creek.

"No," Felicia said, the color creeping steadily up her neck and cheeks. "No, that's not it."

"I told you so!"

He shut the barn door and released his grip on Ingrid. "Now I'm going to give the three of you about two seconds to get off my land. And if I ever catch you back here again, I'm goin' to have the law on you!"

They backed away from him.

"I want you to take a message back to that kid, Merle Steffins!" he shouted. "You tell him for me that I'm giving him his last chance! He's going to have to quit stealing my business or suffer the consequences!"

CHAPTER 6

MORE PROBLEMS

Felicia Cartright and Joan Bailey took Ingrid by the hand and fled. Her tiny fingers were trembling and her palms moist with perspiration. No one spoke until they were out in the road once more.

"Wh–when that Mr. Julian took hold of my arm, I–I was scared," she stammered.

Joan's small mouth firmed. "That's the first time in my life that I ever wished I was a man!" she said between clenched teeth. "He–he got so mad."

Felicia nodded. "I suppose it did make him mad for us to tell him that we'd come over to see if he'd been snooping around the Steffins' place."

"That might be," Joan replied, "but it didn't give him any right to hurt Ingrid the way he did."

They glanced back to see that Dan Julian was still standing there staring at them.

"We–we'd better get going," the smaller girl said, her voice breaking. "He might come after us again."

"We don't have to worry about that," Felicia assured her.

They started up the road once more, but after a few paces, Joan Bailey stopped. "Where's Nosy?"

Felicia and Ingrid both turned to look back toward the Julian cave.

"He was with us just a little while ago," Felicia said.

Ingrid Steffins shuddered. "If that man gets hold of him, there's no telling what he might do to him."

"He won't do a thing to him! He wouldn't dare!" Joan Bailey retorted. She raised her voice. "Here, Nosy! Here, Nosy!"

The little dog did not come.

"Maybe you'd better call him for us, Ingrid. He knows your voice better than he does ours."

The smaller girl called the dog, her shrill voice carrying in the still air. A moment later, Nosy came scurrying from the direction of the barn.

"Git out of here!"

Dan Julian shied a rock at the little dog that hit him on the side and knocked him off his feet.

"That man!" Joan exclaimed. "I wonder how he'd like it if somebody threw a rock at him!"

Nosy scrambled up and dashed on, his short legs flying. Julian threw another rock at him, but by this time, the little dog was out of reach.

Ingrid knelt and swept the little dog into her

arms. "Nosy," she murmured. "Poor Nosy. Let me look at you."

A knot had risen on the dog's ribs where the rock had hit him.

"Oh, you poor dog." There were tears in her eyes.

"I think he's all right," Joan said. "It will probably hurt him for a little while, but he's going to be all right."

Ingrid Steffins put the dog down and stood upright. Anger and defiance blazed in her young eyes. "I can see why Paw hates Mr. Julian!" she said darkly.

Felicia laid a hand on her shoulder. "Ingrid," she said gently, "that's something we must be very careful about. As Christians, we shouldn't hate Mr. Julian or anyone else."

"But he does such *awful* things!"

"We can hate the things he does that are wrong. In fact, we ought to hate them. Jesus hates sin. But we must love the sinner."

Ingrid was hesitant. She looked up at Felicia and then at Joan Bailey. "Do you hate Mr. Julian?" she asked seriously.

Joan was a long while in answering. "You make me very ashamed of myself, Ingrid," she said honestly. "When he hurt you and threw that rock at Nosy I–I'm afraid I did hate him – for just a minute. But we aren't supposed to. As Christians, we have to ask God to forgive us."

Ingrid's small face grew cloudy. "It's hard not to hate a man who's so mean," she said.

"That's right. And without the help of Jesus, we can't do it."

She was thinking seriously. "Will you pray for me so I can feel right toward Mr. Julian?" she asked.

"Of course, we will," Joan assured her.

When they got back to the Steffins' home, the mechanic from Lodgeville was just approaching the disabled Volkswagen. Miss Duncan came flying out of the house and stood looking over his shoulder.

"Do you have any idea what's wrong?" she asked.

He surveyed her critically. "I ain't even had time to look at the engine, lady."

"I beg your pardon. When you have diagnosed the trouble, I want you to explain to me in detail exactly what is wrong and how you will go about correcting it. If this happens again, I want to be able to repair it myself."

Charlie set to work methodically.

"Now why did you do that?" she asked.

It was as though he didn't even hear her. He went right on working.

"Now what are you looking for?" she persisted.

At last, Charlie could stand it no longer. He straightened and turned to face her. "Madam," he said mildly, "did anyone ever tell you that you ask too many questions?"

Miss Duncan flushed a deep crimson. Joan Bailey could not suppress a snicker.

They had lunch soon. Charlie ate with them.

And, as soon as he finished, he excused himself and went back to his job.

"Do you think he's finding out anything?" Joan wanted to know.

"I don't dare ask," Miss Duncan retorted.

It was almost three o'clock when Charlie finally appeared at the door.

"I found your trouble, lady," he said. "Apparently someone was trying to keep you here."

Questions lighted her eyes. "What do you mean by that?"

"Someone took one of the ignition coils. I had a terrible time tracing the trouble."

Her mouth was thin and straight. "Is that a difficult thing to repair?"

"Nope. Ain't no trick to it at all, after we find us a coil for this little 'bug' of yours."

"Don't you have the parts on hand?"

Disgust flickered in his eyes. "Lady, there's more American cars than I can count with parts I ain't even heard tell of, let alone havin' what I need to fix a 'washin' machine engine' like this."

Miss Duncan bristled. "This has been a very trustworthy vehicle for me," she informed him.

"And it will be again as soon as I can find me some place to get that ignition coil."

Miss Duncan calmed quickly. "I'm sorry, Mr.–Mr. Charlie," she said. You will order the part as soon as you can, won't you?"

"Yep." He took the offered olive branch and spoke peaceably. "I'm sorry I can't fix you up this afternoon. But I'll get me that part ordered and as soon as it gets here, I'll come out and put it on for you."

"Thank you." Miss Duncan held out her hand.

He eyed it momentarily, started to offer his own hand, then drew back and wiped it on his greasy overalls.

"Y'know, I take it back about you askin' too many questions, lady. I reckon it just seemed that way."

When he was gone, Miss Duncan called Felicia and Joan off to one side.

"This may be serious," she said guardedly. "Somebody deliberately sabotaged our car to keep us here."

Felicia and Joan stared at one another.

"That explains the screwdriver," the Cartright girl said.

"What screwdriver?"

"The one we found out behind your car." She went and got it. "At the time we found it, we couldn't figure out why it was there."

Miss Duncan took the tool gingerly.

"It must have belonged to the culprit," she murmured thoughtfully.

"We thought perhaps Dan Julian did it," Joan put in, "just to be disagreeable."

"I suppose that is possible," Miss Duncan said, "but it doesn't seem likely to me. Mr. Julian gives every indication of being a very indolent person. I cannot see him stirring himself enough to do something of this sort unless he had a very good reason for it."

"Maybe he has," Felicia Cartright answered.

Miss Duncan's eyes glittered. "What did you say?"

"I said, 'Maybe he has a good reason.'"

"That's what I thought you said."

The girls eyed the older woman curiously. "Do you think you know why he did it?" Joan asked.

"I have nothing more to say." She put the screwdriver in her purse. "I think I will keep this for the present."

They wanted to question her further, but she marched down the stairs and went into the bedroom to visit with Peter Steffins. She was still sitting there some time later when Merle came in from the cave.

"From what I hear, you had a busy day," his father said.

"Yep." The boy dropped wearily to a chair.

"Charlie wasn't able to fix the girls' car," Mr. Steffins continued. "Somebody has stolen one of the ignition coils. He has to order one. It might take a week for it to get here."

"That's too bad."

Mr. Steffins was eyeing him quizzically.

"What's the trouble, Merle?" he asked. "Is there something wrong?"

The dark-haired boy nodded. "There sure is."

Before he could finish what he was saying, Ingrid flew in from the kitchen.

"Paw, Mr. Julian just drove up."

"Dan Julian?" The injured man's face purpled with rage. "What's he doing here?"

"I don't know, but he's getting out of his pickup and coming up the steps."

"Go let him in."

"But Paw!" Merle protested.

"Go let him in!" His voice was harsh.

Merle went into the kitchen in response to the knock and opened the door. Hostility flamed in his eyes.

"Ain't you even goin' to say hello, kid?" Dan demanded, wiping his greasy palms on the bib of his overalls.

"Paw said for you to come in."

"That's right neighborly of you." He waddled into the kitchen, past Felicia and Joan, and into the bedroom. "Good afternoon, Pete. You ought to teach these young'uns of yours to be civil to their elders. It's plumb outlandish the way they treat a body."

"Okay, Julian. What do you want?" Mr. Steffins' voice broke. "Out with it."

"That ain't no way to talk to a neighbor what come over to do you a favor."

Peter Steffins waited.

"I come over to tell you that I'm ready to take this grubby farm of yours off your hands."

"What?"

"I said I'm ready to take over. I'll give you what the place is worth and a little more besides."

"It ain't for sale."

"You don't know what you're saying, Pete."

"I never meant anything more in my life. Now get out of here!"

Merle stood quickly, his temper boiling. "You heard Paw!"

"Simmer down, buddy boy. I don't want to have to get rough with you."

Merle's fists clenched, and he took a step forward belligerently.

"That's all right, Merle. I'll handle it," Mr. Steffins said.

"But, Paw!"

Pete Steffins' voice rose. "I said I'd handle it!"

Dan Julian laughed mirthlessly. "No, you won't. I'll handle it. I come over to give you a chance to realize a little money on this rocky, broken-down farm of yours. But if you don't want to sell it, I reckon I'll have to get it the other way."

"What're you talking about?"

"You ain't paid your taxes for quite a while, Pete," Dan said. "Remember?"

A strange look came to the injured man's eyes.

"My wife was sick for quite a spell, Julian," he said lamely. "And we had a lot of expenses we didn't count on. But I've always paid my bills. I'll get those taxes paid too."

"That's what I came over to tell you," Julian went on, grinning evilly. "You ain't goin' to have to worry about them taxes. I've been paying 'em for you."

Pete Steffins' eyes widened. "What?"

"That's right. I've got the receipts to prove it. Ever' last one of 'em. And when the next one comes due the last of next month and you can't pay it, I reckon I'll have to start the ball rollin' to take over."

Peter Steffins' face was ashen, and when he spoke, anger grated in his voice.

"Get out of here, Dan."

"Sure, I'm goin'. I'm goin'. I know when I'm not welcome. But you just think over what I said. I don't like turnin' you out without no money at all, but if that's what I've got to do, I reckon I'll have to do it."

When he was gone, the injured man seemed to collapse on the bed. He closed his eyes and lay motionless, breathing heavily.

"He was just bluffing, wasn't he, Paw?" Merle asked at last. "Wasn't he?"

Mr. Steffins opened his eyes.

"I reckon not." The strength was gone from his voice. Suddenly, he seemed old and very tired. "He can't take it away from us like that. We'll have a chance to redeem it. But unless we can raise the money he's paid out, plus interest, within a certain length of time, he can take the place over and not give us a penny for it."

Silence gripped the little group.

"If we could only have a good run of tourists next month," he said at last, "I might be able to go to the bank and borrow the money."

The hurt in Merle's eyes deepened.

"We may have to close the cave, Paw," he said numbly.

"Close the cave? Why?"

"Water's coming up in it. That's what I was going to tell you when Dan Julian came in. I couldn't take the last batch of tourists into the Cathedral Chamber. It was full of water."

"I don't see how that could be, Merle," his father answered. "The only time water comes into the cave is in the spring when the snow melts or when we've had lots of rain. And it hasn't rained for several weeks."

"I know, Paw. That's the strange part of it. But it's happening just the same. And, what's more, I'm afraid it's still coming up."

The concern in Peter Steffins' eyes deepened.

CHAPTER 7

A CONFESSION

There was little conversation at the dinner table that evening. Miss Duncan tried several times to engage the others in conversation, but it was useless. The meal was soon over, and Merle got to his feet.

"I think I'll go out and see if the water's still coming up in the cave, Paw," he said.

"That's a good idea." Self-pity filled Peter Steffins' voice. "But at the rate our luck's going, I'm sure it is."

Miss Duncan eyed the dark-haired boy sharply but said nothing.

"I think we'll do the dishes when we come back," she said to Joan Bailey and Felicia Cartright. "Let's go outside for a while."

"I'll do the dishes," Ingrid put in quickly.

"We'll take care of them when we get back," the older woman told her.

"If you weren't here," the girl continued, flashing

a smile, "I'd have to do them all alone and do the cooking besides."

"I'll stay and help you," Joan told her. "Then we'll have them finished twice as fast."

"When they're done, we can go out and see how Nosy is."

Miss Duncan and Felicia stepped out into the still night air.

"Did you have something you wanted to talk to me about?" Felicia asked.

Miss Duncan shook her head.

"No, I want to talk to that young man, and I would like to have you here when I do."

In a few minutes, Merle came out of the cave and walked dejectedly toward the house.

"Young man," Miss Duncan called to him.

He did not slacken his pace.

"Young man!"

He stopped suddenly. "Oh, I'm sorry. I guess I was thinking about something else. I didn't realize you were talking to me."

"Is the water still coming up in the cave?" Felicia asked.

He nodded. "At the rate it's going, it will fill the cave by morning."

"Isn't there any way you could get rid of it?" Felicia asked.

"If we had an expensive pumping system, we could handle it without any trouble," he told her, "but we don't have the money for that, so we'll have to wait until the water seeps away."

He paused momentarily. "What're you doing out here?"

"Waiting to talk to you," Miss Duncan said.

"To me? What about?"

"This." She handed him the screwdriver Felicia and Joan had given her earlier in the evening.

"What kind of a joke is this?" he asked, taking it from her. "What's there to talk about a screwdriver?"

Miss Duncan spoke quietly, but her voice was stern, and her very manner demanded an answer.

"How did this tool get behind my Volkswagen, Merle?" she insisted.

The color faded from his cheeks, but he held his ground. "I haven't the faintest idea."

"Merle!" The word cracked like a whip. "This screwdriver came from your father's tool chest which is kept locked in the shed next to the barn."

"How do you know?" he asked defensively.

"Only you and your father have keys. It's quite obvious that he didn't get up and do it. That leaves you."

"I–I think maybe I left the screwdriver out," he said lamely. "I forgot to put it away."

"As a matter of fact," she told him, "you used this screwdriver to remove the ignition coil from our car, didn't you?"

"I–"

"Didn't you?"

"I–" His voice trailed away.

"Why did you do it, Merle?"

For the space of a minute, their eyes met in the half-darkness of the evening.

"Everything was such a mess here," he blurted at last. "Ingrid did the best she could, but we hardly got a decent meal and there were always dirty dishes in the kitchen, the floors needed sweeping, and the beds weren't made. I figured that if I could keep you three around here for a few more days it would be just that much more that would be done – and that many more good meals we'd have." His voice shook. "I'm awful sorry, Miss Duncan."

She was surprisingly gentle.

"Do you have the coil, Merle?"

He shook his head.

"I was afraid to keep it, so I threw it away." He eyed her in desperation. "Believe me, Miss Duncan, that's the first thing I ever stole in my life."

"I believe you."

Again, all was silent except for the croaking of a frog that blended with the still night air.

"Why would I do a thing like that?" Merle asked. "I knew it was wrong, but I wanted you to stay so bad I did it anyway."

"The Bible tells us why you did it, Merle," she said quietly. "The Bible tells us that we sin because we have sinful natures. In ourselves, we're so weak that we can't keep from sinning."

"Paw always taught me that if I was good enough, I wouldn't have anything to worry about. All I had to do was to do the very best I could."

"But you aren't good enough, are you?" she asked. "No one is good enough now, nor has there ever been anyone good enough to live without sinning. Aside from Christ that is."

"Felicia, here, wouldn't do a thing like I did," he went on. "And neither would you or Joan. Even Ingrid wouldn't."

"That's because we've got Jesus Christ to help us," Miss Duncan said. "Don't you want Him too?"

Merle was breathing heavily. "God wouldn't want me," he said. "I couldn't live up to what he'd expect of me."

"That's the wonderful thing about being a Christian, Merle," she continued. "You don't have to do it in your own strength. God doesn't even expect you to. He not only saves you, but He promises to help you to live the way He wants you to live."

The dark-haired boy grasped her gently by the arm.

"Miss Duncan!" He swallowed the lump that was welling in his throat. "Miss Duncan, I–I want to be a Christian. Will you help me?"

Slowly, carefully she explained the way of salvation, asking Felicia now and then for Bible verses that would explain what she was saying. When at last Merle indicated he understood all that Miss Duncan and Felicia had told him, they knelt with him on the hard, rocky ground. He prayed brokenly for forgiveness.

"I don't know how I can ever thank you," he said at last, getting to his feet.

"You've thanked us enough right now," Miss Duncan said. "Your acceptance of Christ as your Savior has made our whole stay here worthwhile."

Joan and Ingrid came out just then and saw them standing there.

"Oh, there you are," Joan said. "I thought we'd have to look all over for you."

"Do you have something to tell Joan and Ingrid, Merle?" Miss Duncan asked.

His face flushed. "I–I–" His fists clenched nervously. "I just wanted to tell you that I–I'm a Christian now."

"How wonderful!" Joan exclaimed.

Ingrid started to cry softly.

"Ingrid," he scolded, putting an arm around her shoulder. "Stop that blubbering."

"I–I can't help it, Merle. I'm so happy. I've been praying and praying for you."

The next morning, Peter Steffins sent Merle to town to see the banker about borrowing money to pay up the tax bill and keep Dan Julian from taking the farm.

"And if the banker asks you how business is, tell him it's real good; that we're sure we'll be able to pay it back when the note comes due."

The boy hesitated. "But Paw, business isn't good," he protested. "At least, it won't be with our cave full of water."

"He don't have to know that."

"Paw–" The boy fought for words. "If I'm going to talk to the banker, I–I've got to tell him the truth."

His father's temper flared.

"What's got into you, anyway?"

He bit his lower lip.

"Yesterday it wouldn't have bothered me at all to lie to the banker, Paw, but things are different with me now. You see, I'm a Christian."

Peter Steffins stared at him. His lips parted slightly.

"I suppose those girls had something to do with that."

Merle came over to his dad's bed and sat down. "Paw, I used to believe just like you do that if we were good, we didn't have to worry about what would happen to us when we die. I used to think I was as good as anybody. But I found out last night that I wasn't good – that nobody is."

He told him about taking the ignition coil from the Volkswagen.

"You shouldn't have done that."

"It would be just as bad to lie to the banker," the boy said simply.

Mr. Steffins recoiled as though he'd been slapped. "Get to town, then, and do the best you can."

"Paw," Merle said, his voice lowering, "why don't you do what I did last night and accept Christ as your Savior?"

Briefly, the injured man wavered. Then his face hardened, and he looked at the clock.

"You'd better get on your way, Merle. The bank opens at nine o'clock."

Merle Steffins talked to the banker, but it was useless. He refused to loan them the money.

"I'm sorry, Paw," the boy reported, "but he said they've already got a first mortgage on our place and that it isn't valuable enough to warrant a second mortgage."

"I might've known," Pete Steffins said, groaning inwardly. "If I could only have gone to talk with him myself, I think everything would have been all right."

"I did the best I could."

"Sure, you did." Pete reached out his hand and patted his son on the arm.

They were still talking when the news announcer began to tell what was happening out at Dan Julian's Constellation Cave.

"There is great excitement out at Daniel Julian's Constellation Cave today. People have been flocking there in droves since Mrs. Margie Kjar found a ruby that is reported to be worth almost $50,000."

"No wonder all of those cars were in their yard when I went by!" Merle exclaimed breathlessly.

"Shh!" his father hissed. "Let's get the rest of this."

"Remembering that Constellation Cave had at one time in its history been mined quite successfully, Mr. Julian started selling dirt from that portion of the cave at six bucketfuls for ten dollars. The person buying the dirt could keep what he found."

"What a gimmick that is!" Mr. Steffins said under his breath.

"Three days after Mr. Julian started selling dirt, Mrs. Kjar was stunned by her find. 'I wish I'd mined it myself,' Dan said. 'But since I have advertised that I would sell dirt, I am going to continue doing so even if more valuable stones are found.'"

The announcer went on with the news. Mr. Steffins snorted his derision.

"What a racket that is! He'll have suckers from all over the country flocking in there to try to make their fortune."

"Frankly," Miss Duncan put in, "it makes me want to go over there myself."

"Sure. That's the way it affects most everybody." The injured man's agitation increased. "What people don't know is that Dan has bought a cheap ruby in the rough and hired someone to find it. There's a lot of publicity, and the suckers stumble over one another trying to give him their money." He paused and took a long breath. "If I had to make my money cheating people, I'd just as soon go broke."

"I quite agree with you," Miss Duncan said.

"And the worst of it is," he said, "he's getting customers that should rightly be ours. And he's getting them by trickery."

"Except, of course, that we couldn't take care of them now, anyway, Paw," Merle said. "We can't show the cave to anyone as long as it's full of water."

CHAPTER 8

TROUBLE UPSTREAM

That night, in the quiet of their room, Miss Duncan and the girls discussed the situation in which the Steffins family found themselves.

"It seems that every day brings some new development that makes things worse," Felicia said.

"I wish we were rich. We could give them the money to pay off the taxes and put in a pump to pull the water out of the cave."

"But we're not rich," Miss Duncan told them, "so such conjecture is meaningless."

"It's nice to dream," Joan said.

"Daydreaming takes away the initiative," the dean told them, "and makes one less able to deal with realities. A Wellington girl is intensely practical."

She went over and sat down near the window.

"Why do you think Daniel Julian wants to get the Steffins' place?" Felicia Cartright asked at last.

"I think it's because their cave is so much better than his that he finds it hard to compete with them," Miss Duncan said.

"I've never seen anyone quite so determined to get his way," Joan said. "He's really fanatical about it."

Joan pulled back the curtain and looked out at the mountain that was shrouded in darkness.

"I still think all of these things fit together," she mused. "Dan Julian, the tractor tracks, and the flooded cave."

"I don't get it, but I suppose it could be," Miss Duncan said.

"Neither do I – but I'd like to go up the mountain again and see if we can find exactly where that tractor went."

"We did that once," Joan protested.

"It might prove to be profitable," Miss Duncan said. "At least no harm can come from it."

The next morning as soon as the work was done, they went out for a walk, Nosy tagging along behind. Ingrid wanted to go along, but they asked her to stay at the house.

"Are you going over to the Julian place?" she asked fearfully.

"No," Joan explained, "but we're going to try to do something to help your father and you and Merle."

"And you think maybe I might be in the way?"

"Not exactly. We just think it would be better if you stayed at home this time."

"Okay," she smiled quickly, "and I won't say a word to Paw or Merle."

"Good girl."

The girls and Miss Duncan went out to the end of the lane, walked along the highway to the place where the tractor went across the ditch, and followed the tracks.

"They're still plain in some places," Joan said. "But I don't think we're going to be able to follow them when we get up on the hard ground."

"We won't have to follow them," Felicia said. "We know where they went. We can walk right up to the place where they enter the creek."

"That's why I think this is all a waste of time," Joan Bailey countered.

"Maybe. Maybe not."

The short-legged pup ranged alongside, ahead and behind them as they toiled up the mountain slope.

"At least Nosy likes it up here," Joan said. "Now if we could just train him to smell out tractors, we'd really be in business."

"So far we've been able to do all right without him," Miss Duncan said, indicating the tractor tire marks in an occasional patch of soft ground. "But like you say, Felicia, you and Joan know where the tractor went – up to the creek."

"That's the thing that bothers me," Felicia went on. "Where did the tractor go after it reached the creek?"

"We couldn't find out the other day. What makes you think we can now?"

"We've got more time now, and we've got Miss Duncan to help."

They noticed something was different the instant they were close enough to see the mountain stream. Felicia Cartright paused.

"Look!" She exclaimed, pointing with her finger. "This creek is twice as wide as it was when we were here before."

"It is for a fact!" Joan exclaimed. "The water's up around those trees."

"That's strange," Miss Duncan murmured. "That's very strange. It hasn't rained since we've been here."

"No, but I'll bet this high water is causing the cave to flood," Felicia went on. "They said it flooded when the snow melted in the spring and after very heavy rains."

"There must be something that is causing this creek to flood," Joan said.

"That is a very reasonable assumption," Miss Duncan replied. "It is also reasonable to assume that we'll never learn the cause of it by standing here."

She started downstream with long, purposeful strides. Felicia and Joan had to hurry to catch up with her.

"Why are we going this way?" the Bailey girl asked.

"We had to go in one direction or the other," she

said. "Downstream seemed more logical to me since it is in the general direction of the Steffins' cave."

They had walked a couple of hundred yards or so along the swollen creek when Felicia heard something in the trees ahead of them.

"Miss Duncan," she whispered tensely, grasping the dean by the arm. "Did you hear something just now?"

The older woman stopped and listened.

"Should I have heard something?" she asked.

"I do now!" Joan said tensely.

"There's somebody in those trees," Felicia said in guarded whispers.

They crouched, their bodies taut.

"It could be somebody hunting squirrels," the Cartright girl said in an undertone. "Merle said there are a lot of squirrels around and somebody is hunting them all the time."

"Or it could be somebody who drove a tractor up here," Joan observed.

At that instant, Nosy found a gopher and barked wildly at him.

"Nosy!" Joan called, keeping her voice soft.

But it was too late! Whoever had been among the trees went storming noisily out the other side, and all was still.

"Our noisy friend was not a squirrel hunter," Miss Duncan announced with conviction, "or he would not have gone scurrying away at the first sound of someone approaching."

"That dog!" Felicia exclaimed, her disappointment mounting. "Now we'll never know who was in there."

"I–I'm not so sure that I want to know," Joan stammered.

"I'm just glad the guy ran away," Felicia said, "instead of coming over to see what we're doing up here."

"That," Joan told her firmly, "is the understatement of the year."

The girls looked at one another and upstream at the place where they had heard someone running a few moments before. Hesitance and uncertainty gleamed in their eyes.

"Do you suppose that guy kept going?"

"I hope so," Joan said fervently. "I sincerely hope so."

Felicia turned to Miss Duncan. "What do we do now?" she asked, "go on downstream?"

Miss Duncan shook her head. "There are times when it is wisest to retreat. In my opinion, this is one of those occasions."

Felicia glanced over her shoulder reluctantly. "As long as we're here, I would like to see what's causing that creek to be flooded," she said, "but with that man, or whoever it was, up in those trees, I suppose it is best for us to go back home – at least for now."

"Precisely," Miss Duncan said. "A Wellington girl

is brave, but she is also prudent. We will go back down the mountain and return another time."

The other two started down, but Joan still stood there.

"Aren't you coming, Joan?" Felicia called.

"As soon as I get that dog."

"Maybe he went chasing after our friend in the trees."

Joan raised her voice. "Here, Nosy! Here, Nosy!"

"I think he'll be coining along soon, don't you?" Miss Duncan asked.

"I suppose so, but I'd never forgive myself if I lost Ingrid's puppy for her." Joan Bailey turned slowly, her eyes sweeping the steep slope. "I don't see where he could have gone so quickly." She called again. "Here, Nosy! Here, Nosy!"

At last, the pup came running from behind a clump of trees.

"You naughty dog," Joan scolded gently. "Don't you run away again."

"I think we'd better be on our way," Miss Duncan said. "It's getting late, and there's nothing to be accomplished here."

They started down the mountain in comparative silence.

"Do you think we ought to tell Merle and his dad about the creek being flooded?" Felicia asked as they neared the house.

Miss Duncan frowned thoughtfully. "I think it

would be most unwise to tell either of them about it at this point," she said. "In fact, we have very little to tell anybody yet."

They turned in at the lane, and Ingrid came out to meet them.

"Did you find out anything?" she asked, excitement dancing in her eyes.

"Not for sure." Felicia put an arm around her shoulder, and they walked together.

"Can you tell me about it?"

"Not yet. We don't even know if we found out anything that would do any good."

"Oh, I hope so. Paw is so worried."

Near the house, Ingrid paused and glanced around. "Didn't Nosy go with you?" she asked curiously.

"I thought he was right behind me," Joan told her.

"He's probably off chasing rabbits or ground squirrels," Ingrid said. "He does that lots of times."

They went into the house, and Miss Duncan put Felicia and Joan to work getting dinner. Dejection seemed to have taken over the Steffins family. Mr. Steffins and Merle were glum and untalkative as they ate.

"How's the water in the cave?" Felicia asked.

"As high as it's ever been. It fills all except the first chamber now and gives every indication of still coming in."

"It looks as though Dan Julian's going to take over this place after all," Mr. Steffins said. His face darkened. "If we'd get a break – just one break – we could make it."

"The Lord hears our prayers," Miss Duncan said quietly. "Why don't we take the matter to Him and ask His guidance and help?"

The injured man snorted in disbelief. "A lot of good that'll do."

"I've known it to help," the dean said gently. "I've had many, many prayers of my own answered."

"So have I," Felicia echoed.

They bowed their heads, and Miss Duncan, Joan, and Ingrid each prayed. When they finished, everyone seemed to feel a little better. Even the frown on Mr. Steffins' face had softened slightly.

Two or three times while the girls were doing dishes, Ingrid went out to call the dog.

"He's just not around anywhere," she said finally, her concern growing. "He doesn't usually stay away this long."

Felicia turned to Joan Bailey. "I don't remember seeing him since we left the creek, do you?"

She shook her head. "Are you thinking the same thing I'm thinking?"

"The man up there?" Felicia spoke softly.

"If he was Dan Julian, he's just mean enough to do something to Nosy if he could catch him."

"You can say that again."

Joan put aside the dish towel. "I think we'd better go up there and see if we can find that puppy."

"Can I go along?" Ingrid asked.

"Maybe you'd better look for Nosy around here," Joan told her. "Felicia and I will go back where we were this morning and see if he's there."

"You–you'll find him, won't you?" Tears trembled on her eyelashes.

"We'll do the best we can," Felicia said.

Joan Bailey knelt beside her.

"Yes, Ingrid," she promised, wiping the girl's tears, "we'll find him. I love Nosy almost as much as you do. I won't stop until we find him."

Joan and Felicia left the house as soon as possible and retraced their steps up the mountain.

"It would be just like Mr. Julian to catch that pup and take him home," Joan said, her voice sharp with anger.

"I don't know whether he could catch him or not," Felicia said. "You know he threw a rock and hit Nosy with it. I think the dog would remember that and stay away from him."

"I hope you're right. We've got to find Nosy for Ingrid's sake."

They went up to the creek without seeing any sign of the dog. Every now and then, Joan whistled and called to him but without success.

"That's strange," she muttered. "That's very strange."

"You don't suppose Nosy wandered down this way, do you?" Felicia asked, motioning downstream.

A strange glint leaped to Joan's eyes. "You mean

you think Nosy wanted to find out why the creek is so high, the same as you do?"

Felicia Cartright laughed. "Something like that."

"I should've known better than to come up here with you – even to look for a dog. I should've known you'd not be satisfied until you got me over there."

They started to walk along the flooded mountain stream. They had only gone a few hundred yards when they reached a bend in the creek. At the point where it narrowed, a fresh new dam had been thrown up.

"Look! Somebody's built a dam!" Felicia Cartright cried. "That's what's been causing all the trouble."

They approached it curiously.

The dam had been recently built of logs, rocks, and dirt scraped from the upper side. It wasn't well built, by any means, but it did stop the flow of water. The creek was a trickle on the downstream side. Upstream, it was flooding its banks and crawling up around the trees.

"There aren't any crops to irrigate up here," Joan Bailey said. "I don't see why anyone would want a dam up here."

"Neither do I," Felicia said, "unless it was built by Dan Julian to flood the Steffins' cave and put them out of business."

Joan's eyes gleamed. "Felicia!" she cried, "that's it! That's the reason for the tractor tracks and everything. Mr. Julian put in this dam so it would back the water up and create flood conditions. The water must run through cracks and holes in the ground down into the cave when it's above a certain level. Dan Julian would know that and put in the dam to flood Colossal Cave and cause the Steffins family to go broke so they'll lose the cave and the farm to him."

There was a short silence.

"It does all add up at that," Felicia observed thoughtfully. "Only, what're we going to do about it? That's what I want to know."

CHAPTER 9

A DARING PLAN

The girls left the dam and walked down the mountain as quickly as possible.

"What are we going to do?" Joan Bailey asked.

"We'd better talk to Miss Duncan before we say anything to Merle and his father," Felicia Cartright said.

The other girl nodded. "I can go along with that, although I sure don't know what we can do about it ourselves. About getting the thing straightened out, I mean."

Ingrid was still gone when Felicia and Joan got back to the Steffins' house, but Miss Duncan was up in their room.

"She ought to be down in a few minutes," Mr. Steffins said.

"We'll go up and see her," Felicia replied, smiling.

"We'll want to clean up and change clothes anyway after that long walk."

"Did you find the dog?"

"We didn't see anything of him," Joan put in. "We can't figure out what happened to him."

"I wouldn't worry about him if I were you. He just wandered off. He'll be coming home when he's hungry."

Mr. Steffins acted as though he wanted to keep on talking, but the girls excused themselves and went upstairs.

"We found it, Miss Duncan!" Felicia whispered excitedly. "We found out why the creek is high and the cave is flooded."

Hurriedly they told her about the dam.

"We should have known it was something like that," Miss Duncan said. "The water level of a stream doesn't rise without a reason."

"We didn't know what to do," Felicia said.

"Did you say anything to anyone else about this?"

Both girls shook their heads.

"We thought we'd better wait and see what you thought about it first," Joan told her.

"Commendable," Miss Duncan replied. "Very commendable. In a situation like this, we must be sure we're doing exactly the right thing." She expelled her breath slowly. "There is nothing Mr. Steffins can do as long as he is laid up with a broken back, so it would not help any to tell him. And as for Merle,

I'm afraid he is too hot-tempered to trust with such information."

"But he's a Christian now," Felicia answered. "Surely he'll be able to control his temper."

Miss Duncan turned to her patiently. "Felicia," she said, "you would not expect a two-week-old child to feed himself or walk across the room. Neither should you expect a young man with no background in God's Word at all to be able to withstand the temptation in a situation like this."

"If we aren't going to tell them, what are we going to do?"

"Felicia, have you ever heard me say, 'A Wellington girl is equal to any emergency'?"

"Everybody's heard you say that," Joan murmured.

"Exactly. It is almost a motto of the school." Her voice was decisive. "We're going to prove the truth of that motto tonight."

"But how?"

"We're going to remove that dam, of course," she said, as though it was the sort of thing they did every day of their lives. "We're going to allow the creek to go back to normal. That will stop the excessive water running into the cave and flooding it. In short, it will solve one of Mr. Steffins' problems."

"I don't think we can tear out that dam," Joan said. There were big tree trunks and rocks and dirt all mixed in together. It would just be a waste of time trying to get them out ourselves."

"That does create a bit of a problem," she said. "We'll have to think–"

There was a light knock on the door.

"It's me – Ingrid. Can I come in?"

Joan Bailey opened the door to admit the serious faced girl.

"Did you find Nosy?" she asked.

"Not yet."

"I didn't see anything of him either, but Paw says he'll come back."

"I'm sure he will. And, of course, we're not through looking for him ourselves. We may find him tomorrow."

"Oh, I hope so." Her thin voice broke. Then she remembered. "Oh, I was supposed to tell you that–" her voice dropped to a whisper, "that Betty Julian is out behind the barn and wants to talk to you."

"Betty?" Felicia said curiously. "What does she want?"

"I don't know, but she talked like it's real impor-tant." Ingrid glanced about the room as though to reassure herself that no one was listening. "She asked me to go and tell Felicia and Joan to come out and talk to her right away, that she had to see you, and that she had to get back before her uncle knows she's gone."

Felicia picked up a light sweater. "I'm sure it would be all right for you to come along, Miss Duncan."

The older woman shook her head.

"No," she said. "Betty asked to see you and Joan. You two are the ones who should go."

They went downstairs and started for the door.

"Going out again?" Mr. Steffins asked pleasantly.

"Just for a few minutes."

They walked to the edge of the house, beyond the line of vision from Mr. Steffins' bedroom window, and then out to the barn.

"Don't go so fast, Joan," Felicia warned. "If anyone's watching us, we don't want them to get the idea that we're going anywhere in particular."

They went behind the barn and paused.

"Betty!" Felicia called in a hoarse whisper. "Betty!"

"I wonder where she went."

Felicia went to the far corner of the building, but there was no sign of the Julian girl.

At last, the barn door opened a crack, and Felicia and Joan whirled to see a white face and two dark eyes peering at them.

"In here!" Betty exclaimed.

"What's the matter?" Felicia asked.

"In here! Quickly!"

The two girls glanced around and darted into the ramshackle barn. She closed the door behind them.

"Did anybody see you come in here?"

They shook their heads.

"Mr. Steffins is in bed, and Merle's out near the cave doing something or other. We didn't see him, and I know he didn't see us."

"What's this all about?" Joan Bailey demanded.

"My uncle would skin me alive if he knew that I'd come over here," Betty said, fear edging her voice. "But I had to come."

"What's wrong?" Felicia insisted.

Betty Julian's gaze was never still. It darted from one girl to the other, into the far corners of the building, and back to the girls again.

"You don't know what he's like!" she said, shuddering. "But I just had to warn Mr. Steffins and Ingrid and Merle, regardless of what he does to me. I can't let him take everything away from them without warning them."

Felicia grasped her firmly by the shoulders.

"Now, Betty," she said, "slow down and talk sensibly. Start at the very beginning."

The girl took a long, deep breath.

"I heard him and Aunt Mabel talking this morning," the frightened girl said. "They thought I was out in the souvenir shop working. That's the only reason they gave me a home after Dad and Mom died. They wanted someone they wouldn't have to pay to work for them."

"But what about the Steffins family?"

"I'm coming to that. Uncle Dan said that he was doing something to keep Merle from having any tourist business so Mr. Steffins would go broke and he could get their farm."

"Did he say why he wanted it?" Joan broke in.

"I didn't understand what he was talking about, but he said he knows there's another cave on the Steffins' place that's even more beautiful than the one they call Colossal Cave."

"That must be the one Mr. Steffins said his grandfather told him about. Do you suppose Dan Julian found it?"

"He talked as though he knows exactly where it is," Betty said, "but you can never tell about him. He says so many things that aren't true. Anyway, he said he's going to get the farm in his name and open up this new cave. Then he'll get a corner on all the cave business in this end of Missouri – and he'll run all the others out of business and be rich."

Felicia nodded. "We were sure he was trying to run Mr. Steffins out of business," she said, "and we knew he wanted the farm for himself, but we didn't know why."

Fear gleamed in Betty's eyes. "You won't tell him I came over here, will you?" she asked.

"We won't say a word to anyone," Felicia assured.

Betty seemed to relax a little. "I've got to be going. I–I don't know what he would do to me if he found out what I've done."

"We'll be praying for you too, Betty," Joan Bailey told her.

"And thanks a lot," Felicia added.

"Pray that I'll be able to get some other place to

live," the frightened girl continued. "I can't stand it there much longer."

With that, she was gone.

"What do you make of that?" Joan asked.

"I feel so sorry for her. She's so terribly frightened. And I don't blame her. When that uncle of hers gets mad, he'd do anything."

"She's frightened, that's true," Joan went on, "but she's brave too. She came on over here in spite of him."

They went back to the house and up to their room. By this time, it was almost dark outside.

"I'm glad you're back," Miss Duncan whispered. "It's getting so late I was afraid I'd have to go down and start getting dinner before I had a chance to talk to you."

"She found out substantially the same things that we've been suspecting," Felicia said, "and came over to tell us so we can warn Mr. Steffins and Merle."

"If everything goes well, we'll do that very thing – early tomorrow morning."

"What do you mean?"

"Never you mind what I mean. Get downstairs and help me with the cooking and the dishes. And when I say I think it's time to go to bed, get up and go to our room. Do you understand?"

"Why?" Joan asked curiously. "What will we do then?"

"Suppose you wait and find out," Miss Duncan said archly.

The evening meal dragged on endlessly or so it seemed to Felicia and Joan. But at last, they finished eating and had the dishes done. Miss Duncan visited amiably until about nine o'clock, when she got to her feet.

"Well, I think I'm going up to our room," she said significantly. "How about it, girls? Are you coming along?"

"It's early yet," Merle protested.

"I know, but I think it would be best. We've had a long, hard day."

"I wish I could say the same," he retorted, bitterness creeping into his voice. "But I haven't done anything except to watch the water creep higher in the cave."

"Perhaps that situation will change soon," Miss Duncan informed him.

Once the girls and Miss Duncan were in their bedroom and the door was shut, Felicia and Joan pounced on her.

"Now, what're we going to do?" Felicia demanded. "What's this all about anyway?"

"As soon as the others go to bed and the house is quiet, you'll find out."

Felicia and Joan both knew that it was a waste of time to question Miss Duncan further. When she was ready, she would tell them her plans and not before. They got out their Bibles, had devotions together, and crawled into bed.

The three of them lay in their beds, staring up into

the darkness. They could hear the muffled tones of voices in the room below them and the occasional sounds of footsteps crossing the floor. But at last, the house was quiet. Felicia listened, her young body tense with excitement and expectation. Half an hour passed since they had the last indication that someone was still up. Only then did Miss Duncan get out of bed.

"Girls," she said crisply, "girls, it's time."

Joan, who had dozed off a moment before, sat up and scrubbed the sleep from her eyes.

"Time for what?"

"Dress quickly," Miss Duncan said. "We have much to do."

Felicia stooped to put on her shoes.

"How are we going to get out of the house without being heard?" she asked.

"Our window opens onto a porch," Miss Duncan informed her, "and the porch is graced with a sturdy rose trellis. I questioned Ingrid thoroughly and am convinced that it's strong enough to hold us."

They dressed in the dark, and Joan opened the window.

"I'd still like to know where I'm going and what I'm going to do," she mumbled.

"For the moment you are going to carry this," Miss Duncan said. She handed Joan Bailey a small roll of something that was a bit thinner than a clothesline.

"And you, Felicia, can put these in your pocket, but be very careful of them."

She handed Felicia two small brass objects that looked very much like the casings for rifle bullets.

"What're these?"

"Just be careful of them," Miss Duncan said. "I will carry this."

Felicia Cartright's eyes widened and her mouth sagged open as she saw what Miss Duncan had in her hand.

"D–d–dynamite!"

"Dynamite?" Joan echoed. "Wh–wh–what're we going to do with that?"

Miss Duncan was very calm and matter of fact.

"How else are we going to move that dam that's causing so much trouble?"

"You–you aren't serious about blowing it up with dynamite, are you, Miss Duncan?" Felicia asked.

"Most assuredly. It is very simple to use. No harder than preparing a cake with a cake mix. I've read the directions half a dozen times. Three sticks of dynamite taped together and properly detonated should clear out the dam very efficiently."

"Have you ever set off dynamite b–b–before?" Joan Bailey asked.

"Joan," she said, "I have managed to keep the lid on a school of girls for more than twenty years. Setting off a charge of dynamite does not seem at all formidable, let me assure you."

"Where did you get the dynamite?" Felicia asked. "That's what I can't figure out."

"Every farmer in this part of Missouri has dynamite around – or almost every one of them. They use it to blast out stumps, rocks, and that sort of thing. Ingrid is my co-conspirator. She got the dynamite, the fuse, and the caps from the supply her father keeps in the attic of the barn."

"Well," Joan Bailey put in, her voice betraying her nervousness, "it's been nice knowing you, Miss Duncan. At least we will be able to say that we were there when it happened."

"Nonsense." The dean crawled out the window onto the porch roof and beckoned the two girls to follow her.

CHAPTER 10

THE EXPLOSION

Miss Duncan climbed down the rose trellis, and Joan and Felicia followed her. Once they were all on the ground, the dean led them across the yard, past the barn, and up the steep mountain slope in the direction of the dam.

"It's awful dark, Miss Duncan," Joan Bailey said solicitously. "Would you like to have me take your arm?"

"I'm quite capable of walking by myself, thank you."

"B–but you stumbled back there."

"It didn't hurt me a bit."

"I know," Joan said, "but I sure don't want you to fall down. Especially when you're carrying that dynamite and are walking so close to me."

They stopped to rest.

"Girls," Miss Duncan said, "I have one small favor to ask of you."

"In case you make a mistake setting off that dynamite, you mean?" Joan asked.

"Not exactly." She drew in a deep breath. "We faculty members are not subject to the dictates of the school during our summer holidays," she said, "but if word of this evening's caper were to get back to Wellington, I would have quite a difficult time explaining it to the girls and the authorities."

"You don't have to worry about a thing," Joan Bailey said. "If we live through it, we'll never say a word about it to anyone."

"Thank you. My conscience is entirely clear in the matter. This is something we must do, but I would appreciate discretion on your part."

The moon was only a slice in the sky, but there was enough light from it to take the edge off the darkness. Once their eyes were accustomed to the night, they were able to pick their way up the slope with ease. After a time, they reached the dam.

"Now what do we do?" Felicia asked.

Miss Duncan hesitated but only for an instant.

"The directions say to place the dynamite under the object to be moved." She studied the dam carefully. "This would appear to be the logical location."

She got to work, feverishly pulling aside sticks and digging in the sand to get the dynamite under the dam.

"Now tamp sand or dirt around it," she said.

"B–but not too hard!" Joan Bailey cautioned.

"That sounds like a good way to get that stuff to go off before we're ready."

When the dynamite was in place, Miss Duncan called to Felicia. "Force the end of the fuse Joan is carrying into the dynamite cap you have in your pocket and hand it to me."

Numbly, Felicia did as she was told.

"About all we need now is for Dan Julian to come around," Joan said.

"You can think of the most pleasant things."

"About all we need now," Miss Duncan said, "is a match."

"A match?" Joan echoed. "Don't you have a match?"

"I was so concerned about getting the dynamite and learning how to use it," Miss Duncan admitted sheepishly, "that I forgot we would have to get a match to light the fuse."

Felicia was fishing in her jacket pocket.

"Wait a minute," she said. "I think I've got a match here." She pulled out a match with the stick broken in half. "It's not going to be easy to use."

"It will do," the dean said. "It will do."

Before she lit the match and touched it on the fuse, she asked Felicia to lead them in prayer, and they bowed their heads. Felicia prayed for their safety and for the success of their venture. Then Miss Duncan struck the match. The fuse sputtered.

"Run!" she cried. "Run!" Felicia and Joan dashed madly away. Miss Duncan did the same. Thirty feet from the dam, she caught her toe on a root and went sprawling, but she scrambled up and dashed on. They ran until they could run no more.

"Is–is this far enough away?" Joan panted.

"I–I don't know," Miss Duncan sputtered. The directions didn't say anything about–"

"Whoom!" The blast rocked the earth around them and threw rocks and dirt and logs into the air. Briefly, it rang in their ears.

At last, the dust began to clear away.

"It worked!" Felicia shouted exultantly. "It worked!"

Sure enough, the water was pouring over the remnants of the dam.

"We can thank God for that," Miss Duncan said.

It was two or three minutes before anyone spoke again.

"I just thought of something," Joan said at last. "We were going to keep this a secret from Merle and his dad until tomorrow morning."

"And what's wrong with that?" Miss Duncan asked.

"Nothing. Only it's going to be a good trick after all that noise."

"That reminds me of something else," Felicia put in. "Dan Julian's probably heard it too. We'd better get out of here."

They started down the hill, when they heard a faint yelp from somewhere in the distance.

"Nosy!" Joan cried.

"That did sound like him," Felicia added.

"Of course, it's him. I'd know that bark anywhere."

They looked around but could see nothing.

"Here, Nosy!" Joan called. "Here, Nosy!"

After the first faint barking, they heard no more.

"Here, Nosy!"

"We'd better get back to the house, Joan," Felicia said. "If Merle and Mr. Steffins find out we're gone, they're going to be worried silly."

"But I can't leave until we find Nosy."

"We can't find him in the dark," Miss Duncan countered. "We know about where we are now. We can come back in the morning and make a thorough search of the area."

"He might not be here in the morning."

"That's a chance we'll have to take." Miss Duncan became the dean again. "We must hurry, girls. Already it is past our bedtime."

They left the mountain stream at the place where the dam had been and walked briskly down to the Steffins' farmstead. When they got near enough, they saw that the house was ablaze with lights.

Merle met them on the porch. "There you are!" he exclaimed. "We've been worried about you."

"We're quite all right, thank you," Miss Duncan informed him.

"Somebody set off a charge of dynamite. It sounded as though they blew the whole top off the mountain."

Miss Duncan went into the living room and sat

down. "No," she told him. "It was only large enough to blow out the dam in the creek."

"Dam?" Merle echoed. "What dam?"

"The dam Mr. Julian built in the creek to flood your cave."

Understanding gleamed in his eyes.

"So that's why our cave filled with water. I thought it strange when it's been so dry."

"I don't know how long it will take for your cave to empty itself of water," Miss Duncan went on, "but at least there will be no more coming in from that source."

"And who set off the dynamite?" Mr. Steffins called from his bedroom.

"The girls and I. Why?"

"You could have killed yourselves." There was reproach in his voice.

"We were very careful," she told him. "We followed the instructions to the letter, and everything went according to plan. You see, Mr. Steffins, Wellington girls are trained to meet emergencies."

"But how did you find the dam? That's what I'd like to know."

Starting at the beginning, they told how they had seen the tractor tire marks, followed them up the mountain to the creek, and finally located the dam.

"I guess we have much to thank you for." He sighed deeply. "If it isn't too late already."

"What do you mean?"

"I've been checking things over in my mind all evening," he said. "We owe so much and have so little time to get it paid that I don't see how we can make it. I'm afraid we wouldn't even have been able to make it if we hadn't had the mine fill with water." His gaze lowered slowly. "It looks to me as though Dan Julian may have beaten us anyway."

"Oh, no!" Felicia exclaimed.

"Not that we don't appreciate the efforts you girls have made to help us," he said quickly. "We'll never forget you. Believe me."

"But there must be some way of managing without losing everything."

"If there is, we'll find it," he told her. He meant the statement to reflect optimism, but it only underlined his deep dejection.

Soon the girls went up to bed.

"I thought that all of Mr. Steffins' troubles would be over when we blew up that dam," Felicia said as the door closed behind them.

"So did I," Joan added.

"That was our way of solving things," Miss Duncan said. "Perhaps God has something else in mind."

"I don't know." Felicia was heavy-hearted. "It doesn't seem to me that there's any answer for them. No matter how hard I try, I don't see any way out."

The following morning, everyone in the Steffins' house was up an hour before they usually were. By the time breakfast was ready, Merle had been down to the cave and back again.

"The water's dropping all right," he said. "It looks as though it's gone down a couple of feet already."

"That's good news," Miss Duncan said.

"Yes, in a couple or three days, I think we'll be able to start showing tourists through it again."

Mr. Steffins said nothing, but it was apparent that the news had not wiped away his worries.

"I don't know about the rest of you," Merle said, sitting up to the table, "but I'm going up and take a look at that dam Miss Duncan and the girls blew up." He grinned infectiously. "I'll bet old Julian roared when he heard that explosion last night."

"You want to be careful going up there this morning, son," Peter Steffins warned. "You know Dan as well as I do. He'll likely head for the mountain himself to see what happened."

"I can take care of myself."

"That's not what I'm afraid of," Mr. Steffins told him.

"I don't care about seeing where that old dam was," Ingrid put in. "I want to find Nosy."

"And we're going to look for him until we find him," Joan promised her.

They left the house and headed for the mountain stream where Dan Julian had built the dam. As they walked, they fanned out, keeping a sharp watch for the little dog and calling out for him from time to time. They were almost to the place where the dam had been built when Ingrid Steffins cried out suddenly.

"Listen!"

For an instant all was silent – breathlessly so.

"What are you hearing?" Felicia asked.

"Listen!" the little girl said again tensely. "It sounds like someone crying."

"Oh, that," Felicia replied. "I heard that noise last night when we were up here, but I didn't think it was anything special."

"It's Nosy!" Ingrid exclaimed. "I know it is!"

"It sounds as though it comes from over this way," Joan said. She veered sharply to the left. "I don't see him anywh–" The word choked in her throat. "Here he is!"

"Where?"

The others crowded around her.

Joan pointed to a small hole in the ground. "He must be down there!"

They couldn't see the little dog, but there was no mistaking where he was. As he heard their voices, he began to bark loudly.

Ingrid dropped to her stomach and peered into the inky darkness.

"Nosy!" she said over and over again, half crying. "Nosy! Nosy!"

Joan tenderly put a hand on the girl's shoulder.

"Don't worry, honey. We'll get him out."

CHAPTER 11

AN EXCITING DISCOVERY

We'll have to go back to the house and get a shovel and some rope," Merle Steffins said. "That hole's going to have to be dug out a lot larger."

"Do you think you can get him out of there?" Joan asked. She was as concerned as Ingrid. "We can't even see him."

"We ought to be able to manage it after we get something to work with." He started away. "I'll be back as soon as I can."

"What kind of a hole is this anyway?" Miss Duncan asked curiously. "It looks as though it could have been dug by a badger or some other burrowing creature."

But Merle wasn't there to answer her. He had already gone striding down the mountain.

Ingrid had not moved from her vantage point beside the hole since they had found where the dog was.

"Now don't you worry, Nosy," she said. "We're going to get you out of there."

As she talked to him, the puppy whimpered plaintively.

While they were waiting, Miss Duncan and the girls went up to the mountain stream. There was a large hole where the dam had been, and the flow of the creek was reduced to normal.

"It looks as though we took care of that situation all right," Joan remarked.

"If only the rest of the Steffins' problems could be solved so easily," Felicia Cartright put in.

It wasn't long until Merle Steffins was back, jouncing over the rough, stony ground in the pickup.

"You'll have to get back so I can get to work, Ingrid," he said. Before starting to dig, he lay on his stomach beside his younger sister and pointed a flashlight down the hole. "Wow!"

"Do you see him?" Ingrid asked.

"Sure, I can see him, but he's down there a long way."

"Is–is he all right?"

"He looks to be. He's sitting on his haunches right below us, looking up at us."

"The poor little guy." Ingrid's voice broke. "We'll have you out in just a little while, Nosy." She turned to her brother. "You'll be able to get him out, won't you, Merle? Won't you?"

"I'll do the best I can. Now, you're going to have to get back so I can work."

Joan took Ingrid by the hand and drew her a few steps to one side.

They all watched silently as Merle Steffins began to dig. For half an hour or so, he worked in the hard ground. The sweat glistened on his face and soaked his shirt. Every now and then, he stopped to rest.

"Do you think you need help, Merle?" Miss Duncan asked after a time. We could go to one of your neighbors and get them to come over."

"The only neighbors we've got who live close are Dan Julian and his wife, and I don't think Dan'd be apt to come over here." He laughed dryly. "I wish I were a little smaller. I believe I could get down there now."

"Would you like to have me try?" Felicia asked.

He surveyed her critically.

"It's quite a way down," he said. "Are you sure you wouldn't be scared?"

"I'd probably be scared," she admitted, "but I think I could do it."

Merle looked at Miss Duncan. "Is it all right?" he asked her.

"Would you be able to do it, young man?" she asked.

"Oh, sure!"

"Then Felicia can. A Wellington girl is able to do most things a man can do."

"Okay." He picked up the rope. "We'll have to put

this around you so we can let you down to where the dog is."

Felicia was very nervous but said nothing as Miss Duncan placed the rope under her arms and tied it securely.

"Goodbye, dear friend," Joan said. "It's been nice knowing you."

"Now you're going to be a lot of help," Felicia muttered.

Felicia Cartright took the flashlight from Merle and let herself into the hole. The others grasped the rope and braced their feet to keep her from falling.

"All right! Lower away!" A moment or two later the rope slackened. "I'm down!" she called. "Now to switch on the light and–" She didn't finish what she was saying.

The silence was breathless.

"Felicia!" Joan Bailey cried. "Are you all right?"

"Oh!" she gasped. "Oh!"

"What's the matter?" her best friend repeated fearfully.

"It–it's magnificent!"

"Whatever are you talking about?" Miss Duncan demanded.

"This is the most beautiful place I've ever been in my whole life!" Felicia said, awe tinging her voice. "There are colored ribbons and spikes and–and all sorts of beautiful shapes down here – everywhere you look!"

"This must be the cave my great-grandpaw used to tell paw about!" Merle exclaimed, his voice trembling.

"That could scarcely be possible," Miss Duncan protested, "unless your great-grandfather was considerably smaller than I think he was. He could never have gotten down in that hole."

"There's probably another entrance somewhere else," the boy told her. He directed his attention to Felicia once more. "Are there any passages leading out of that chamber?"

"I–I think so," she said uncertainly. "It looks to me as though there are several."

"Why don't you get the dog and come up?" he said. "I want to go tell paw and get someone to help explore this thing."

Felicia Cartright came up in a moment or two, her face still reflecting the excitement of what she had discovered.

"I was never so surprised in my life," she said. "I switched on the light to find Nosy, and I could scarcely believe what I was seeing."

The others were standing around her breathlessly. All, that is, except Ingrid. She had swept the puppy into her arms and was squeezing him tightly. Tears coursed down her cheeks, but she didn't even know she was crying.

* * *

Later that morning, Merle went into town and brought a couple of his friends out to help him open the hole larger and go down into the cave.

"It's all Felicia said it was and more, Paw," he told Mr. Steffins that night. "There are dozens of rooms and passageways that are so much more beautiful than our other cave that I can't even find the words to compare them. It—it's simply magnificent!"

Mr. Steffins' smile came from his heart.

"That's the best news we've had in weeks," he said. "But from the way my grandpaw used to talk about it, I knew it must be something wonderful." He paused briefly. "How soon do you think you can have it so you can take Mr. Grainger from the bank down to have a look at it?"

"I could show it to him tomorrow if he wanted to be lowered on a rope the way we were."

Peter Steffins laughed. "I think maybe you'd better wait until you build a good, sturdy ladder and get the hole cut bigger. After all, we've got to borrow money from him to get our bills paid and to open this cave. We don't want to scare him to death before we get it."

"I don't think there'll be any question about getting the money, Paw," the boy went on. "Anybody would loan us money if they could see what we've got. Why, we're going to have people flocking in here from all over the country. It'd be worth driving a thousand miles just to see the part of the cave we saw this afternoon, and we only got in a little part of it."

"Now you sound like Dan Julian," his dad said mildly.

"But I'm telling you the truth. I can hardly wait until your back's better so you can go down and take a look at it yourself."

Mr. Steffins nodded. "I know the bank will loan us the money," he said. "I've already talked to Mr. Grainger about this new cave. He told me over two years ago that if I ever located it, they would be glad to advance what we'd need to get it opened up to the public."

Miss Duncan and the girls served coffee and sandwiches. When Joan finished asking the blessing, Merle sat up straight.

"Oh, yes," he said, turning to Miss Duncan, "before I forget it, when I was in town picking up the guys this afternoon, I stopped in at the garage and got the coil for your car. It came this morning. I'll put it on for you tomorrow."

"Thank you, Merle," she said. "I'm glad to have it. I have an errand to attend to tomorrow."

The next morning, Ingrid helped with the dishes.

"Are–are you going to be leaving today?" she asked.

"No," Miss Duncan said quietly. "I have something else to do today. We'll get away in the morning."

"You–you'll feed Nosy good, won't you?" Ingrid said. "He got so hungry and thin down in that cave. I've been feeding him special."

"That's something we want to talk to you about," Joan Bailey put in. "I think we'll leave Nosy with you."

"But–but I gave him to you," the girl protested.

"I know," Joan said, "and we'd *love* to take him with us. But you see, we live in a big dormitory with a lot of other girls, and they don't allow us to keep dogs."

"Maybe they'd let you keep Nosy." She looked at Miss Duncan appealingly. "He isn't like the other dogs. He's different."

"They couldn't let us keep a dog," Joan continued. "If they did, all the girls would want to keep their cats and dogs at school, and it would make a terrible nuisance." Joan smiled down at her. "Nosy is so used to being out in the country where he can run and play that he wouldn't be happy in town. And we wouldn't want that, would we?"

Ingrid shook her head solemnly.

"Besides," Joan went on, "if you have Nosy here, that will be one more reason for us to come back and visit you."

The younger girl beamed.

"I–I'll keep him for you and take care of him just as though he's my very own. And if you ever want to take him, you can."

"It's a deal." Joan thrust out her hand impulsively.

Miss Duncan had said no more about her errand that morning, and Felicia and Joan thought she had forgotten it, but when the dishes were done, she went upstairs for a light sweater.

"Come on, girls," she said. "We might just as well get it over with."

"Where are we going?"

"I'll tell you about it on the way."

She pulled out of the yard and turned in the direction of the Julian place.

"You aren't going over to see Dan Julian, are you?" Joan asked.

Miss Duncan shook her head. "Definitely not."

"I'm thankful for that."

"I'm going over to see that poor girl who is staying there."

The girls both gasped.

"What?"

"I'm going over to see Betty Julian."

"Why don't you just stop and let me out here?" Joan said. "You can pick me up when you come back – if you come back."

"Nonsense!" Miss Duncan turned in at the sign. "I have yet to see a man I'm afraid of."

Daniel Julian was in the souvenir shop when they drove up and stopped. He came out on the step and glared at them. Miss Duncan paid no attention to him.

"Come on, girls." She opened the car door. "We don't have much time to spare."

Numbly, Felicia and Joan did as they were told.

"You, there!" Mr. Julian bellowed. "Get back in that car and get yourselves off my place!"

Miss Duncan did not slacken her stride. "We will do that very thing," she told him quietly, "as soon as we've completed our business here."

"You ain't got no business here, and you ain't wanted. Now git!"

He stepped over to block her path.

"Move aside, my good man."

"I said, beat it!"

Her best dean-of-Wellington stare met the anger in his eyes.

"I said, move aside," she repeated. "I have some business with your niece."

She came up a step, and he moved backward, grumbling.

"You nosy females! All you do is stick in where you've got no business to."

Still, he made no move to stop them. Joan and Felicia pushed gingerly past him.

"Now mind you," he called as Miss Duncan went inside, "I want you out of here. You ain't welcome." He thought for a moment and flung open the door. "Betty – don't you sell 'em nothin'. Don't sell 'em a thing–" He considered what he had said. "'Less they pays cash."

Fright stood in Betty Julian's eyes. She came over to her visitors.

"I–I'm sorry for the way he acts," she apologized.

"You don't have to apologize for him," Miss Duncan said. "We came over to see you."

"Me?"

"I've been thinking about you, Betty. You haven't finished high school, have you?"

She shook her head. "And it doesn't look as though

I'm going to get to. I'm going to have to work to support myself."

"That's what I came to talk to you about. How would you like to come to Wellington School?"

"Oh, I'd love to." The light in her young face died. "But I could never afford to go there."

"I think it can be arranged," Miss Duncan said, smiling. "We have a scholarship fund at Wellington for girls like yourself."

Betty was incredulous. "You–you mean I could go there and–and be with Felicia and Joan and the other girls?"

"If you'd like to and your uncle will let you."

"If he'll let me?" she echoed. "I'm not his ward. The court didn't place me here. I can leave anytime I want to. I talked to a lawyer. He said Uncle Dan can't stop me."

"That's fine. Splendid."

"It's wonderful!" Felicia Cartright said with feeling.

"You can come with us to California," Miss Duncan said, "or you can come to school in the fall."

Decisively, Betty took off her apron and laid it on the nearest counter. "I'll go now. Wait until I get my suitcase. It won't take but a minute."

"Should you give your uncle any notice before you go?" Miss Duncan asked.

"I don't think I have to. He hasn't been paying me, and when I asked him about it and told him what the lawyer said about my leaving if I wanted to, he said I could go anytime."

Felicia and Joan looked at one another excitedly. Betty was going with them – and right away! Things were happening so fast they didn't seem real.

* * *

That evening was their last at the Steffins' home. Miss Duncan and Joan fixed a big meal, and Felicia and Betty did the dishes afterward.

"You know, Miss Duncan," Pete Steffins said. "The most wonderful day of our lives was the day you girls drove into the yard. Things are going to be different in our family and our home from now on."

"There's another day that could be even more wonderful to you," she said. "That would be the day you trusted Christ as your Savior."

Briefly, silence gripped the little group.

"That's what I was talking about," he said. "Through you and the girls, Merle became a Christian, and this morning while you were all gone, he got to talking to me about it. A little while ago, I confessed my sin and got straightened out with God."

Miss Duncan could not speak immediately. She looked over at Felicia, whose eyes had suddenly filled with tears.

"How wonderful!"

"It's been a thrilling time for us too," Felicia Cartright said softly. "And now, it's even more thrilling."

Joan Bailey and Betty Julian didn't say anything, but it was obvious to look at them that their hearts were full.

THE
FELICIA CARTRIGHT
SERIES

Felicia Cartright, a petite blonde who is one of the most popular students at Wellington School for Girls, has a surprising inclination toward mysteries. If a mysterious situation arises, it either makes its way to Felicia, or Felicia somehow finds it. Though this is a bit trying for her happy-go-lucky roommate, Joan Bailey, it does prevent life from becoming monotonous. It also enables Bernard Palmer, the popular author of the "Danny Orlis" books, to write an entertaining series of stories for girls aged twelve to eighteen.

The mysteries range from a valuable missing antique to an attempt by claim jumpers to steal a deposit of tungsten ore. There's excitement and action galore—but there's also spiritual guidance and blessing because Felicia and her partner-in-adventure love the Lord and take Him into account in all their experiences.